THE COMPLETE GUIDE TO
FLOWER ARRANGING

The Complete Guide To
FLOWER ARRANGING

JANE PACKER

DORLING KINDERSLEY
LONDON · NEW YORK · STUTTGART

A DORLING KINDERSLEY BOOK

Photography
Dave King

Project Editor
Stefanie Foster

Art Editor
Tracey Clarke

Editorial Assistant
Nell Graville

Designer
Helen Diplock

D.T.P. Designer
Karen Ruane

Senior Editor
Susannah Marriott

US Editor
Ray Rogers

Managing Editor
Rosie Pearson

Managing Art Editor
Carole Ash

Production Manager
Maryann Rogers

*Dedicated to my wonderful family for all that they do,
especially Gary, Rebby, and my little Lola*

First American Edition, 1995
2 4 6 8 10 9 7 5 3 1

Published in the United States by
Dorling Kindersley Publishing, Inc.,
95 Madison Avenue,
New York, New York 10016

Library of Congress Cataloging-in-Publication Data
Packer, Jane, 1959–
Complete guide to flower arranging/by Jane Packer. – 1st American ed.
p. cm.
Includes index.
ISBN 1-56458-868-8
1. Flower arrangement. I. Title.
SB449.P2214 1995
745.92–dc20 94-31858
CIP
Reproduced in Italy by GRB Editrice, Verona
Printed and bound in Italy by A. Mondadori Editore, Verona

CONTENTS

INTRODUCTION 6

THE PRINCIPLES OF FLOWER ARRANGING 8

ARRANGING FRESH FLOWERS 26

INTRODUCTION

I HAVE SPENT ALL MY WORKING DAYS with flowers and feel fortunate
to be surrounded by their beauty and freshness most of the time.
I began working in a florist's shop at the age of 15 and what started
as means to earn a bit of pocket money developed into a fascination
with and lifelong love of flowers. I couldn't believe what could be
done with flowers and how much detail, passion, and hard work
was involved in their preparation.

In this small shop in a small town, during an era in which most
people would never consider buying flowers for themselves, floral
arrangements were sold mainly for birthdays, anniversaries,
weddings, and, ultimately, funerals – the major milestones in life.
Today, things are different: people **do** buy flowers solely for themselves,
and on a regular basis, too. Many supermarkets include flowers
within their range of usual products and produce, making them more
accessible to most people, and although the current range of flowers
they offer may sometimes be limited, it is growing rapidly. And with
an ever-increasing selection of blooms and foliage available, the
hunger for whatever the "new look" may be is constantly growing, too.

During my career I have worked in all areas of the flower industry,
and I have often found a reticence among my colleagues to share their
skills and information with the general public. Some florists feel that
by selling florist's foam to customers and showing them how to

arrange flowers, they may endanger their own livelihood. I believe this attitude is wrong. To encourage people to arrange flowers more often and to experiment with and enjoy the myriad varieties available means they will buy more flowers, demand different varieties, and expect longer-lasting and better-conditioned blooms. This has to be good both for the flower industry – an industry I feel passionately about – and for the pleasure people derive from flowers. In 1989 I opened a school of flower arranging in London. Since its beginning, I have met many people who have a wonderful eye for color and a real love of flowers, but who are desperate for more information and guidance on what to do with flowers. They long to escape from the rigid, formal teaching that many have experienced with traditional exponents of "floral art," toward a more day-to-day and realistic approach. They come to my school because they want to achieve with flowers a look that is natural, uncontrived, and easy to live with. These ideas embody my philosophy of flower arranging, and I have aimed to demonstrate them in this book.

There have been many beautiful, inspirational books published on the subject of flowers and there will, of course, be many more in the future. What I believe this book can offer is a precise insight into how to choose flowers and work with them. From a simple posy to the trickiest bridal shower bouquet, I have tried to explain the mysteries involved with simple instructions and clear step-by-step photographs. I hope these practical projects improve your flower arranging technique and inspire you to experiment with your own ideas.

Jane Packer

The Principles of Flower Arranging

The inherent properties of the flowers and foliage you decide to use should always set the style of an arrangement, establishing its dominant color, shape, and texture. While traditional flower-arranging techniques provide useful guidelines, I do not consider them as rigid rules. It is far more important to express yourself and create a display that sits comfortably in its setting.

STYLES OF ARRANGEMENT

WHEN STARTING an arrangement, consider whether the eventual setting of the display calls for a formal, modern, or casual theme. Then think about the container you plan to use and which flowers will enhance its size, shape, color, and texture. Here, all the containers are made of galvanized metal, but each one has a distinct style and will be displayed in a different setting, so the results look quite diverse.

POTTED DISPLAY
Planted arrangements are most striking when kept simple. A single ornamental cabbage needs no adornment to create impact in a simple galvanized jug, and suits a variety of settings.

CLASSIC FORMAL DISPLAY
Strong lines and a sparing use of flowers suit a clean, formal setting. These roses impart classic grace to a tall vase with a suitably sharp outline.

COUNTRY-STYLE ARRANGEMENT
*A random variety of red and orange flowers
and foliage presents a casual, unstudied
display in a country-style jug, perfect for
an informal location.*

MODERN GROUPED ARRANGEMENT
*Small, unusual containers grouped together
and filled with one type of flower make a
stylish, innovative arrangement for a
contemporary backdrop. Here, the containers
are as important a feature as the flowers.*

DRIED CORNCOBS form the backbone of the arrangement

FLOWERS AND PLANT MATERIAL are massed in groups by type

SMALL TERRA-COTTA POTS are secured by pushing a cut stem from one of the plants through the base into the dry foam

THICK CORNCOB STEMS are cut
on a slant to make them easier
to push into the dry foam

LARGE INFORMAL DRIED ARRANGEMENT
*The lack of movement and suppleness in dried
flowers means they risk appearing stiff and spiky
if used sparingly. To avoid this, mass the flowers
together by type, keeping the arrangement compact
and bold. Massing flowers in groups not only
intensifies their colors and exaggerates textural
contrasts, but also recreates the way they
grow naturally, which is particularly
appropriate for a casual setting.*

DEEP PURPLE LARKSPUR lift
the arrangement, contrasting
vividly with the rich yellow
sunflower heads

GNARLED SUNFLOWER LEAVES,
saved from the stems,
provide interesting
textural contrast

LOW TERRA-COTTA BOWL
packed with dry foam

LARGER STALKS OF TIMOTHY hang
over the edge of the container

CHOOSING FRESH FLOWERS

FRESH FLOWERS TRANSFORM A ROOM with their beauty, color, and scent. Select stems partly in bud to last longer, and, if combining flowers, try to mix varieties of similar longevity. Bold, eye-catching flowers provide the focal point for an arrangement, while less conspicuous blooms act as filler and recessionary material.

CALLA LILIES
The classical elegance of these beautiful flowers marks them out for more grand or formal displays, as well as modern arrangements.

DELPHINIUMS
Long, supple delphiniums add height and movement to large-scale displays. As cut flowers, delphiniums are expensive, but they can be homegrown in favored areas.

CORNFLOWERS
Cornflowers have a country-style simplicity in casual displays, and also suit compact, massed arrangements. The bold color and round shape is ideal for boutonnieres.

DARK PURPLE CORNFLOWERS impart strong color and depth

HYDRANGEAS
Large, bushy hydrangeas are useful for massing together. They have a good color range and look effective fresh-cut or dried.

Calla lily
Zantedeschia

JUST TWO OR THREE stems are enough to make an impact

DELPHINIUMS come in blue, purple, white, and pink shades

BUSHY, YET DELICATE, the heads are helpful for compact displays

Cornflower
Centaurea cyanus

Mop-headed hydrangea
Hydrangea macrophylla

Delphinium
Delphinium

DAHLIAS
Lush dahlias make a strong statement when mixed together in a display of clashing colors.

PREVENT SILKY BLOOMS from drooping by adding flower food to the water

ROSES
The beauty, scent, and romance of roses make them the most popular of fresh flowers. Choose blooms that are not yet fully open.

ASTILBE
Light, feathery astilbe form the perfect complement to heavier flowers. They range in color from white to cream and pink to dark red.

THE STRONG SHAPES and bold colors of dahlias make for a good focal point

ASTILBE should be used in combined displays as a foil for heavier flowers

Pink
Dianthus plumarius

WAXY, DARK ROSE LEAVES – a good choice for filler foliage

Dahlia
Dahlia

Rose
Rosa

Astilbe
Astilbe

PINKS
Traditional and long-lasting, pinks are smaller than carnations. They have a sweet scent and suit table displays and boutonnieres.

ENCOURAGE NEW BUDS to open by removing old flower heads

CHOOSING FOLIAGE

ALMOST EVERY ARRANGEMENT includes foliage, whether on the flowers themselves, or as a separate ingredient. Foliage is used in displays as filler material, or to add textural and color contrast. Stronger, bold pieces can be used to form the outline of an arrangement, while longer, supple foliage adds width and a sense of movement.

EUCALYPTUS
An extremely versatile type of foliage, eucalyptus in its many varieties works as beautiful filler material for all sorts of arrangements.

FLOWER HEADS add movement and highlights of color

FLAT, SMOOTH LEAVES complement larger, defined flowers

ENGLISH IVY
A popular, year-round foliage, English ivy softens any display with its trailing lines. A wide range of leaf sizes comes in plain green and variegated patterns.

ROSEMARY
Supple lengths of rosemary spill out effectively from a display, while short stems are good fillers.

ROSEMARY provides a delicious scent and silvery tones

TENDRILS OF ENGLISH IVY impart a flowing quality to arrangements

HOSTA
A smooth surface and strong leaf shape make this variety ideal for the base of displays, or as edging to larger bunches.

Eucalyptus
Eucalyptus

English ivy
Hedera helix

Hosta
Hosta fortunei
'Aureomarginata'

Rosemary
Rosmarinus officinalis

BUPLEURUM
This country-looking foliage is a pleasing filler that provides color contrast with its soft lime green flowers.

BEAR GRASS
A fine classical foliage, this grass is best used sparingly with architectural flowers such as lilies and amaryllis for a modern, minimalist feel.

Bear grass
Dasylirion

STRONG, FLEXIBLE STEMS add flowing lines and minimalist elegance to simple displays

BUTCHER'S BROOM
There are several different types of Ruscus, *and they all last up to four weeks. The variety featured here lends a soft, arching quality to taller displays.*

COPPER BEECH
A summer foliage, copper beech should not be used too early in the season since its new leaves are soft and wilt quickly. The strong copper color is a valuable alternative to green foliage.

Shrubby hare's ear, Bupleurum
Bupleurum

DARK MAHOGANY LEAVES are useful for color contrast and as filler foliage

SMOOTH, SHINY, supple stems create a strong structure

Butcher's broom
Ruscus aculeatus

Copper beech
Fagus sylvatica
f. *purpurea*

CHOOSING DRIED FLOWERS

DRIED FLOWERS allow you to create year-round, permanent arrangements, but because many of them are brittle and lack natural movement and suppleness, you must plan the finished display thoroughly before starting to arrange. To compensate for the flowers' rigidity, aim to use them in fairly compact displays with a definite outline, and avoid single protruding stems. Always handle dried flowers carefully.

GOLDEN CORNCOBS add color and texture to modern or rustic arrangements

CORNCOBS
The glowing color and rough husks complement grasses, seedheads, and autumn-colored flowers in harvest displays. To dry corncobs, secure chicken wire horizontally, and support the cobs upright in the gaps.

GLOBE ARTICHOKES
Beautifully shaped globe artichoke heads are arresting whether displayed singly or combined with other dried vegetables.

ROSES
With the wide variety of roses available, one type can be found to suit every kind of display. Cut stems before the blooms have fully developed, and dry with the heads apart (see page 183).

ROSE BLOOMS retain their scent after drying

DRIED LAVENDER imparts deep color and scent to small and large-scale displays

Corncob
Zea mays

HEAVY, SCULPTURAL HEADS of globe artichokes look striking in large-scale displays

Globe artichoke
Cynara scolymus

Rose
Rosa

Lavender
Lavandula spica

LAVENDER
Tiny, mauve lavender flowers emit a sweet, delicate scent that lasts for months after drying. For best results, bunch lavender stems together in small posies.

SUNFLOWERS
The size and color of sunflowers suit them to both sophisticated and country-style displays. The flowers can be massed, either on the stems or cut down, and the leaves also provide interesting dried foliage.

THE BOLD, CHEERFUL COLOR and distinct shape of sunflowers make them a dramatic focal point flower

Sunflower
Helianthus

AMARANTHUS
The supple stems of fresh amaranthus become poker-straight when dried. Its lime green and rusty red flowers impart warmth and texture to summer and autumn displays.

POPPY PODS
Oval-shaped and smooth-surfaced, poppy pods combine well with richly colored flowers and foliage. Spray paint the pods for use in more festive displays.

Poppy pod
Papaver

SMOOTH, MAUVE-GRAY poppy pods give structure and a distinctive shape to many types of display

VELVETY SPIRES soften textural arrangements

VIBRANT-COLORED circular heads are available in a wide spectrum of colors

Amaranthus
Amaranthus

Strawflower
Helichrysum bracteatum

STRAWFLOWERS
The compact, rounded heads of strawflowers look striking when massed together. They have weak stems, so often need to be wired.

COLOR SCHEMES

COLOR IS THE PREDOMINANT FACTOR in any arrangement, and while the style of display and range of flower forms play an equal part in the finished piece, color makes the initial impression. It is important to experiment with different tones, and to mix and match shades. Do not be afraid of testing new color combinations – even traditional "clashes" of color can look impressively vibrant.

BOLD RED DAHLIAS impart a rich opulence

RIBBON is used to pick out the color of the dahlias

DEEP BLUE DELPHINIUMS contribute depth

PURE YELLOW ROSES have a vibrant, luminous quality

PRIMARY COLORS
Bringing the primary colors on the color wheel – blue, red, and yellow – together in an arrangement creates a strong color scheme. By just softening each tone, the overall effect would be more subtle.

MAUVE SCABIOSA form a
link between the lilac-
colored delphiniums and
purple cornflowers

LILAC DELPHINIUMS are
a lighter shade of the
primary blue color

MONOCHROMATIC SCHEMES
*A monochromatic color scheme uses shades
of the same color. Here, a range of blues,
including both strong and delicate shades,
forms a harmonious blend.*

VIOLET LISIANTHUS
complement the primary
vibrant yellow of calla
lilies and marigolds

COMPLEMENTARY COMBINATIONS
*In the color wheel, each secondary color is the
complement of the one primary not used in its
makeup, and combining the two can look
striking. Here, violet (formed from red and blue)
is mixed with its missing primary, yellow.*

BALANCING CONTAINERS AND FLOWERS

THE CONTAINER IS INTEGRAL TO THE DESIGN of a flower display, and
its size, shape, color, and texture all affect the choice of flowers
and determine the final effect. When container and flowers
are sympathetic to one another, the display is
seen as one object. Clear glass containers
almost disappear in a display, making
them appropriate for most settings,
while colored or textured containers
will always have a more significant
influence over the choice of flowers
and can be linked to their
surroundings more emphatically.

LOW-LEVEL DISPLAY
*Here, I have disregarded the
traditional rule of using flowers
at least twice the height of the
container, but the compact
group of full, round ranunculus
complements the simple
container perfectly.*

MASSED FLOWERS
*A massed group of delicate fairy-
tale-like lachenalia sets off this
squat, square tank, below right.
Using one variety of flower en
masse, rather than a mixture,
presents a cleaner, bolder
statement of modern simplicity.*

CLASSICAL MODERNITY

Single stems of roses are ideal for the classic, clean look of this tall, cylindrical container. A display of this height should be viewed from the side, but larger, more open blooms could be cut quite short and placed in a low bowl display to be viewed from above.

RUSTIC JUG

A mixture of flowers and foliage clustered tightly together, below left, in a casual arrangement creates lots of natural charm. When grouped with the matching bowl, the containers form a lovely country composition.

NATURAL DISPLAY

This warm Provençal bowl intensifies the oranges in the flowers. The mixture of flowers, foliage, and herbs suggests that they have been gathered and displayed on impulse.

ACID GREEN EUPHORBIA breaks up the clashing reds, pinks, and oranges of the flowers

THE CHOICE OF FROSTED GLASS transforms an essentially country-style display into something suitable for a modern setting

DRAMATIC CONTRAST

*Flowers saturated with vibrant color are a superb
foil for this cool, frosted white bowl. Grouped in a
random patchworklike display, they spill over the
bowl in a profusion of color, their stylized
extravagance echoed in the parrot tulips
casually strewn alongside the bowl. The
dramatic effect is enhanced by
deliberately keeping the
display as low as possible.*

INTRICATELY FORMED rich pink
parrot tulips contrast with the
color and texture of the bowl

HEAVIER BLOOMS hang over
the edge of the bowl, giving
extra width to the display
and a feeling of abundance

ARRANGING FRESH FLOWERS

Fresh flowers should not be confined to festivals or celebrations. The presence of flowers can subtly alter the atmosphere of a room, introducing a sense of calm and bringing natural freshness and color indoors throughout the year. The projects that follow create different moods and encompass many styles of display, from a sophisticated centerpiece to a simple basket planted with spring bulbs.

ROUND TABLE DISPLAY
This luxurious arrangement uses a wide variety of flowers arranged by type to create a natural, informal look.

FOAM-BASED ARRANGEMENTS

EVERY ARRANGEMENT OF FRESH FLOWERS has its own unique style, often inspired by a special occasion, the decor and period of a room, or current fashion. Whether formal, homey, or modern, the finished style can be as varied as the selection of flowers that make up the display, and florist's foam is invaluable in helping to create the effect you wish to achieve.

This traditional material is one of the conventions of floristry that I still use extensively. When soaked in water, it is ideal for creating natural-looking fresh flower arrangements in almost any shape or size of container. By supporting the flower stems and allowing them to draw off as much water as they need, the foam acts in much the same way as soil.

Balance of form is central to any successful arrangement, and florist's foam helps to achieve it, allowing you to place flowers so that the height of a display is proportionate to its width. The final position of an arrangement also affects its impact; foam enables you to angle the flower heads to suit a display viewed from above, placed against a wall, or centered on a table. Flowers cut on a slant can also be easily positioned in foam to face in various directions and create gentle, curved outlines. This is useful when making front-facing displays and wreaths, or hiding a container behind trailing flowers and foliage.

Foam-based arrangements do not last as long as freestanding displays in fresh water, but you can prolong their life as much as possible by pushing stems toward the center of the foam (taking care not to cross them) to prevent the foam from crumbling, and by adding water daily. To make sure the foam is thoroughly soaked, do not submerge it in water, but let it float on the surface. This allows the water to be absorbed all the way through the foam, and not just around the sides.

Front-facing Display
Page 30

Hurricane Lamp Ring
Page 36

Round Centerpiece
Page 40

Basket Arrangement
Page 44

FRONT-FACING DISPLAY

WHEN MAKING A FRONT-FACING display, think of it as a "half-round" arrangement, aiming for soft curves and natural groupings of flowers. One common mistake is to position all the stems in one direction. Avoid this by ensuring some flowers lean backward. This prevents the display from looking front-heavy and falling forward.

DESIGN TIP
The display should be broadly triangular in shape, but allow some longer stems to break the outline to soften the effect.

20in (50cm)

24in (60cm)

MATERIALS AND EQUIPMENT

If you wish, replace the flowers listed here with the same quantity of other flowers of a similar size and shape.

Flowers and foliage

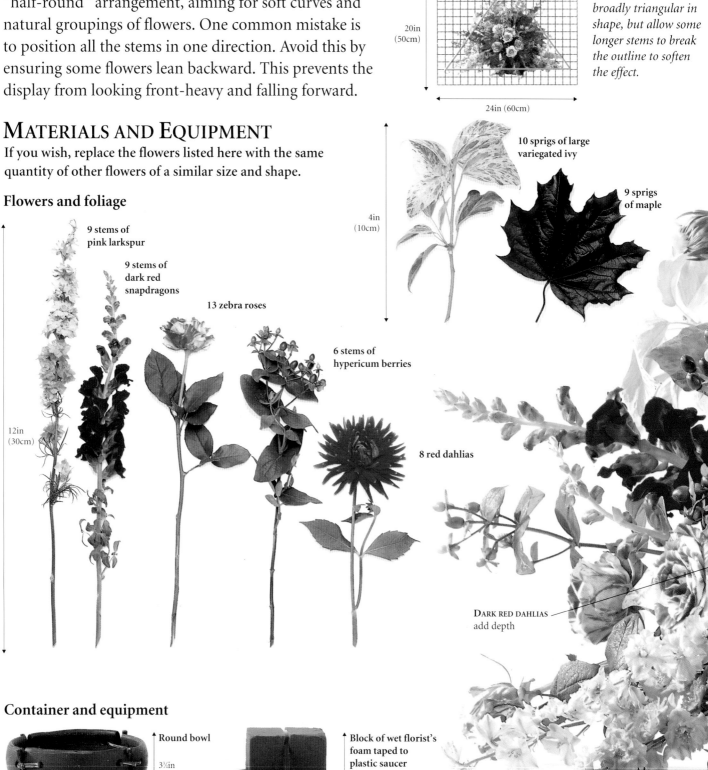

9 stems of pink larkspur

9 stems of dark red snapdragons

13 zebra roses

6 stems of hypericum berries

10 sprigs of large variegated ivy

9 sprigs of maple

4in (10cm)

12in (30cm)

8 red dahlias

DARK RED DAHLIAS add depth

Container and equipment

Round bowl

3¾in (9.5cm)

8in (20cm)

Block of wet florist's foam taped to plastic saucer

4¾in (12cm)

6¼in (16cm)

PALE PINK LARKSPUR set the height

SIDE VIEW
Create a full triangle with some stems placed to fill in the back of the display, as shown.

DELICATE HYPERICUM BERRIES fill in spaces

RED SNAPDRAGONS continue the outline

THE FINISHED EFFECT
A rich and sumptuous arrangement in toning shades of red and pink, backed by contrasting light and dark foliage.

CONTRASTING IVY AND MAPLE provide filler foliage

ZEBRA ROSES grouped for a natural effect

MAKING THE DISPLAY

First prepare the flowers and foliage (see page 174).
Place the foam in the container up to about 1in
(2.5cm) higher than the rim. The techniques shown
here can be used for seasonal variations on the same
style of arrangement (see pages 34–35).

POSITION UPRIGHT
stems to fan out
slightly, and side stems
to point forward,
sideways, downward,
and upward.

ADD FLOWERS to the sides
and front in groups
of three

GROUP STEMS in
threes for impact

*1 Push stems of larkspur into the top of the
foam at the back, and into the sides, in groups
of three. Stems in each group should be of
different lengths. Angle the side stems downward,
and vertical stems slightly backward.*

*2 Add the snapdragons in
groups of three next to each group of
larkspur, at different lengths within each
group. Make sure they do not break the outline
created by the larkspur.*

PLACE THE ROSES centrally,
and to the sides

*3 Add zebra roses as a focal point. Group
seven shorter-stemmed flowers deeper
and more centrally in the display, and
add three longer-stemmed roses to each side,
at different lengths and sloping downward.*

ZEBRA ROSES provide
the main focal point

Side view

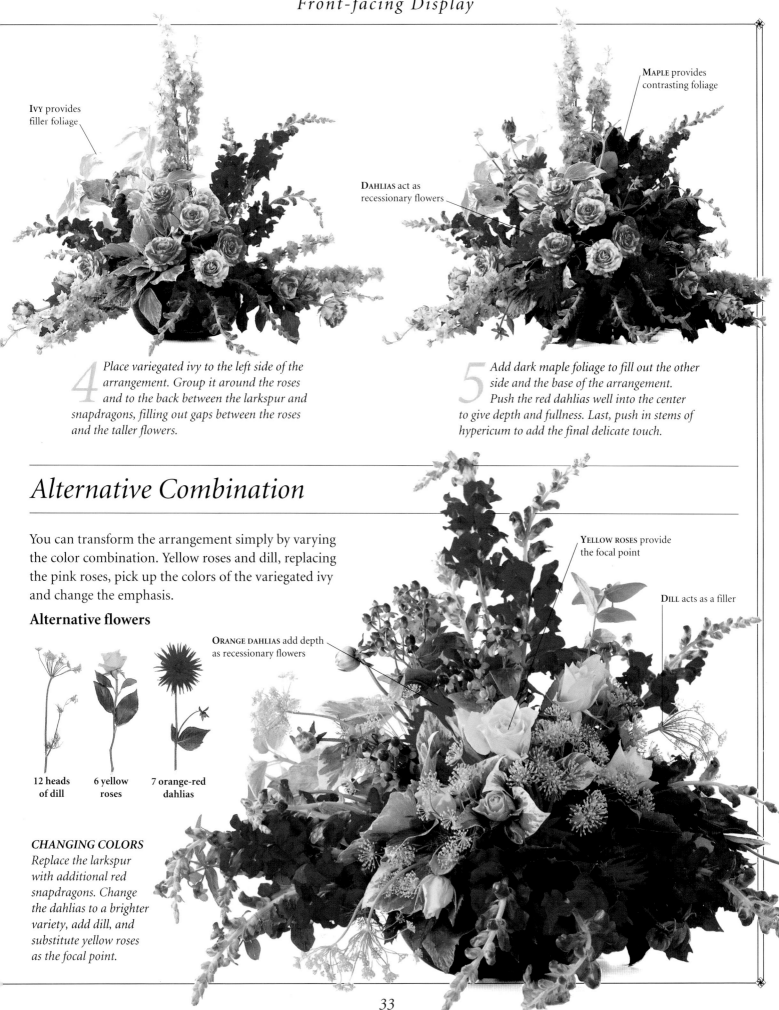

IVY provides filler foliage

MAPLE provides contrasting foliage

DAHLIAS act as recessionary flowers

4 Place variegated ivy to the left side of the arrangement. Group it around the roses and to the back between the larkspur and snapdragons, filling out gaps between the roses and the taller flowers.

5 Add dark maple foliage to fill out the other side and the base of the arrangement. Push the red dahlias well into the center to give depth and fullness. Last, push in stems of hypericum to add the final delicate touch.

Alternative Combination

You can transform the arrangement simply by varying the color combination. Yellow roses and dill, replacing the pink roses, pick up the colors of the variegated ivy and change the emphasis.

Alternative flowers

12 heads of dill

6 yellow roses

7 orange-red dahlias

CHANGING COLORS
Replace the larkspur with additional red snapdragons. Change the dahlias to a brighter variety, add dill, and substitute yellow roses as the focal point.

YELLOW ROSES provide the focal point

DILL acts as a filler

ORANGE DAHLIAS add depth as recessionary flowers

Winter Display

Adapt the principles used in the front-facing display on pages 30–33 to produce an opulent arrangement for mid-winter celebrations such as Christmas. Leucadendron stems are pushed into the back and sides of wet florist's foam, followed by larger foliage, twigs, and roses, arranged asymmetrically for a natural effect.

VELVET-TEXTURED ROSES are placed through the center of the display, providing the main focal point

DELICATE RED SPRAY ROSES echo the color of the larger crimson roses and add depth

BARK is pinned onto the florist's foam to start the arrangement

STEMS OF LEUCADENDRON set the height and width of the arrangement

VARIEGATED HOLLY leaves provide filler foliage and soften the triangular outline

DOGWOOD TWIGS break out of the triangular outline on both sides of the display

RUGGED BARK introduces a coarse texture and evokes the countryside

HURRICANE LAMP RING

CREATING A RING OF FLOWERS around a central feature is an interesting exercise in floral design. Since candlelight, coupled with a rich array of flowers, is an ideal evening decoration, here I have chosen to work with a hurricane lamp. To maintain impact, ingredients are kept simple.

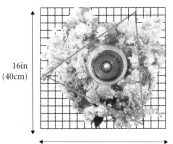

16in (40cm)

16in (40cm)

DESIGN TIP
Flowers and foliage are placed at three equidistant points around the ring, and the vibrant heads of achillea punctuate the circle of flowers and moss. This systematic approach ensures a well-balanced, yet natural-looking display.

MATERIALS AND EQUIPMENT

All flowers and foliage are pushed directly into the wet foam, and only the moss requires floral wires to hold it in place.

Flowers and foliage

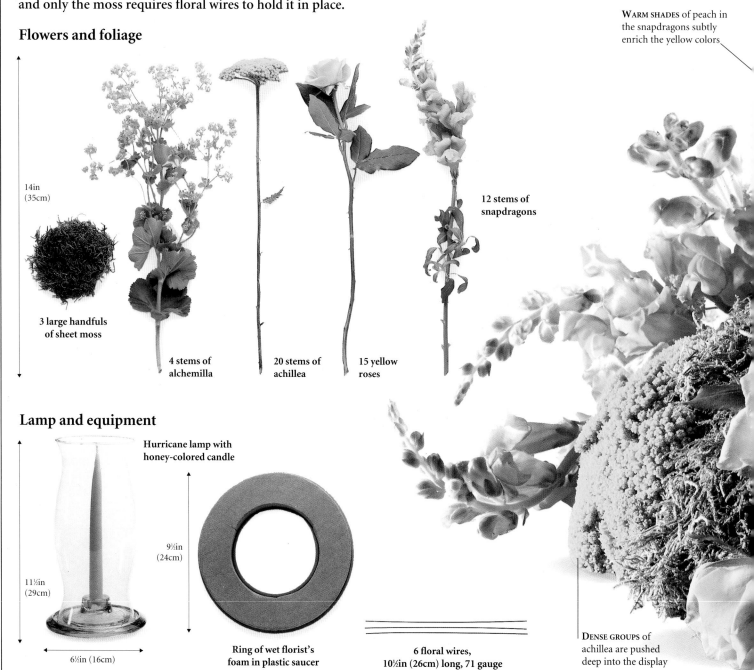

14in (35cm)

3 large handfuls of sheet moss

4 stems of alchemilla

20 stems of achillea

15 yellow roses

12 stems of snapdragons

WARM SHADES of peach in the snapdragons subtly enrich the yellow colors

DENSE GROUPS of achillea are pushed deep into the display

Lamp and equipment

Hurricane lamp with honey-colored candle

11½in (29cm)

9½in (24cm)

6½in (16cm)

Ring of wet florist's foam in plastic saucer

6 floral wires, 10½in (26cm) long, 71 gauge

THE FINISHED EFFECT
The natural curves of the snapdragon stems add a sense of movement to an otherwise compact arrangement.

THE HURRICANE LAMP
sets the height of the decoration

SUPPLE SNAPDRAGONS
extend farthest from the ring, contributing movement to the display

YELLOW TIPS of alchemilla are highlighted by the vibrant yellows surrounding them.

ROSES are the main focal flower

MAKING THE RING

Foliage and flowers are attached in
groups on the wet foam ring. Each type
of material forms a separate group,
creating a compact, natural effect.

**ANGLE LONGER
LENGTHS** down
from the sides
and up toward
the lamp

ATTACH THREE GROUPS
of moss at equal distances
around the ring

1 *Put the hurricane lamp in the center of the
wet foam ring in the saucer. Cut the floral
wires in half, bend into hairpin hooks (see
page 177), and hook on the handfuls of moss
at three equally spaced points around the ring.*

2 *Cut shoots and leaves from the alchemilla
to 2–4in (5–10cm) in length. Push first the
leaves, then groups of buds into the foam
between the moss. Push shorter stems in deeper
and keep them in the center of each group.*

3 *Trim the achillea stems to about 2½in
(6cm), and push them into the foam in
groups between the sections of moss and
alchemilla. Push the heads in deeper than the
alchemilla, keeping them level with the moss.*

KEEP THE ACHILLEA
flower heads level
with the moss

PUSH IN ACHILLEA on
either side of the moss

4 *Cut the leaves off the roses and trim the stems to 2in (5cm). Divide the leaves into three separate groups, then the heads. Push groups of leaves, then flowers between the alchemilla and moss. Finally, trim the snapdragons to 6in (15cm). Add in three groups around the ring.*

MAKE SURE the roses stand out above the achillea, but are below the level of the alchemilla

LET LONGER LEAVES extend from the base of the ring

Alternative Combination

The mood has been changed here by substituting subtly tinted flowers for warm, sunny yellows and by selecting a pastel green candle.

Alternative flowers and foliage

6 mauve mop-headed hydrangeas

12 shoots of senecio

15 stems of lisianthus

MOP-HEADED HYDRANGEAS replace the achillea

TRAILING SENECIO takes the place of the snapdragons

FRESH TONES
Purple-tipped lisianthus, hydrangeas in various shades of pink and purple, and senecio replace the roses, achillea, and snapdragons. A muted green candle complements these new colors, and the overall effect is more delicate.

LISIANTHUS FLOWERS are substituted for roses

ROUND CENTERPIECE

USING TRADITIONAL FLOWER-ARRANGING techniques, I have arranged flowers and foliage symmetrically to build up a display on foam that gives the impression of a triangular posy. Vibrant orange poppies and tulips are grouped by type, their bold shapes and color softened by delicate narcissi and bushy hebe.

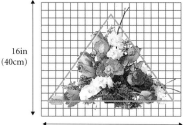

16in (40cm)

24in (60cm)

DESIGN TIP
While the arrangement is round, it looks triangular from the side. Twigs, flowers, and foliage are pushed into the florist's foam in equally spaced groups around the sides, establishing the circular shape and overall symmetry.

MATERIALS AND EQUIPMENT

No special container is needed for this arrangement. It is built up on florist's foam taped to a saucer, and the flowers and foliage cover both almost completely.

Flowers and foliage

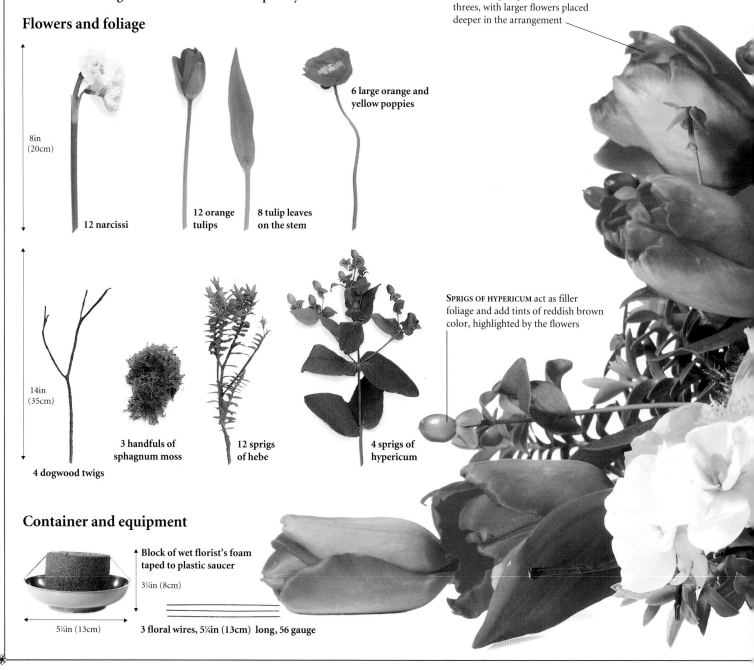

8in (20cm)

12 narcissi

12 orange tulips

8 tulip leaves on the stem

6 large orange and yellow poppies

14in (35cm)

4 dogwood twigs

3 handfuls of sphagnum moss

12 sprigs of hebe

4 sprigs of hypericum

TULIPS are grouped in twos and threes, with larger flowers placed deeper in the arrangement

SPRIGS OF HYPERICUM act as filler foliage and add tints of reddish brown color, highlighted by the flowers

Container and equipment

Block of wet florist's foam taped to plastic saucer

3¼in (8cm)

5¼in (13cm)

3 floral wires, 5¼in (13cm) long, 56 gauge

DOGWOOD TWIGS break
out of the outline and
enhance the natural look

DELICATE NARCISSI visually lift the
arrangement, the yellow centers
highlighting the poppies and tulips

THE FINISHED EFFECT
*While the symmetry of the display gives
a slightly formal quality, the overall
effect is cheerful, casual, and rustic.*

TWIGS introduce a
rustic element and
emphasize the red
hues in the flowers

MAKING THE CENTERPIECE

First prepare the flowers and foliage (see page 174).
Set the height and width of the arrangement
with the dogwood twigs. The rest of the
flowers and foliage are grouped by type
around these points.

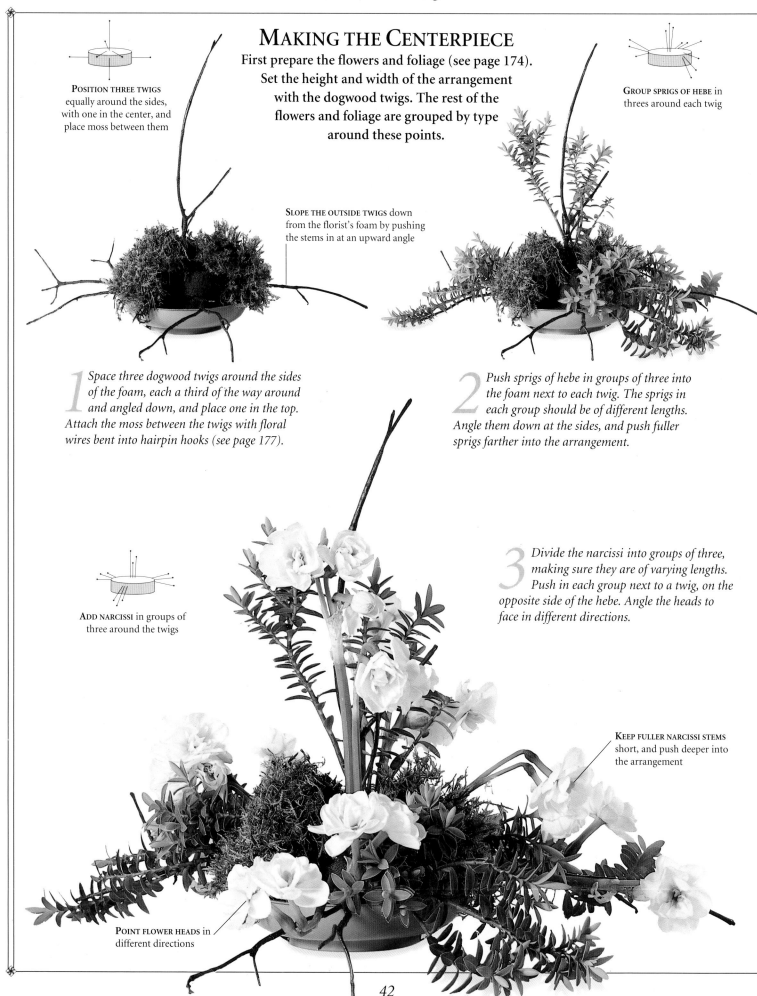

POSITION THREE TWIGS equally around the sides, with one in the center, and place moss between them

SLOPE THE OUTSIDE TWIGS down from the florist's foam by pushing the stems in at an upward angle

GROUP SPRIGS OF HEBE in threes around each twig

1 Space three dogwood twigs around the sides of the foam, each a third of the way around and angled down, and place one in the top. Attach the moss between the twigs with floral wires bent into hairpin hooks (see page 177).

2 Push sprigs of hebe in groups of three into the foam next to each twig. The sprigs in each group should be of different lengths. Angle them down at the sides, and push fuller sprigs farther into the arrangement.

ADD NARCISSI in groups of three around the twigs

3 Divide the narcissi into groups of three, making sure they are of varying lengths. Push in each group next to a twig, on the opposite side of the hebe. Angle the heads to face in different directions.

KEEP FULLER NARCISSI STEMS short, and push deeper into the arrangement

POINT FLOWER HEADS in different directions

4 Add tulips in groups of two or three. Push them in at different lengths, keeping larger blooms deeper in the arrangement. Push in cut-off stems with leaves still attached next to the flowers.

Luscious large poppy heads act as recessionary flowers

Tulips are added to the sides and top in groups of two or three

Push in separate tulip stems with leaves next to the flowers

5 Place the large orange and yellow poppies deep and more centrally within the arrangement to fill it out. Finally, push in sprigs of hypericum at different lengths among the groups of flowers.

Longer tulip stems slope down from the sides

Alternative Combination

Substitute hyacinths, anemones, and English ivy for the tulips, poppies, and hypericum for a completely different yet equally bold color combination. You may even like to try combining the orange and purple colors for a really stunning result.

Alternative flowers and foliage

9 purple hyacinths

12 purple anemones

12 sprigs of variegated English ivy

Hyacinth heads replace the tulips

BLUE THEME
For a less springlike, yet just as dramatic effect, replace the orange flowers with deep purple anemones and hyacinths. Place larger, more open flowers toward the center of the display.

Variegated ivy is substituted for the reddish hypericum

BASKET ARRANGEMENT

THE BASKET ARRANGEMENT has become a popular request for florists. Baskets themselves appear in many guises, and fashion trends ensure that their shapes and the materials used to make them constantly change. Here, I have used a very traditional basket, round in shape with a good depth to fill with florist's foam.

MATERIALS AND EQUIPMENT

To prevent water from leaking out, a plastic bowl is placed in the basket with the wet florist's foam secured with tape.

Flowers and foliage

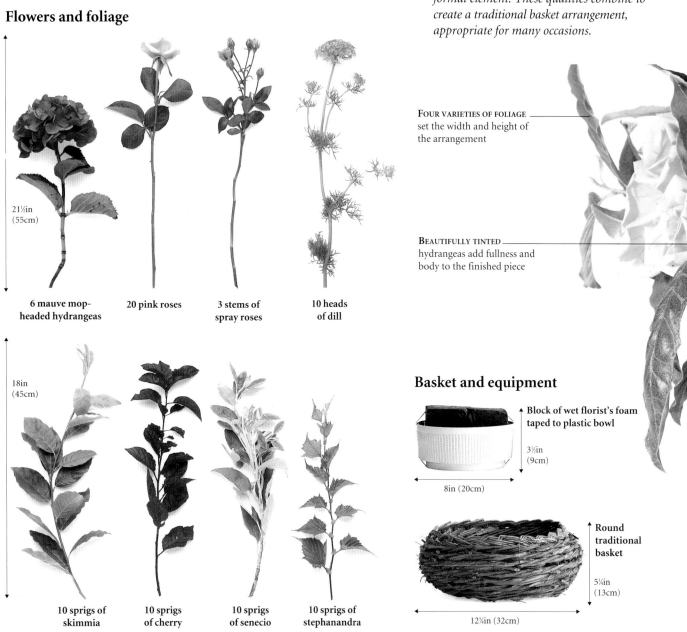

16in (40cm)

18in (45cm)

DESIGN TIP
The flowers and foliage have been positioned to follow the form of the basket. They mirror the flat, rounded shape, creating the impression of a sphere.

THE FINISHED EFFECT
Mop-headed, country garden-style hydrangeas and dill complement the rustic basket, while classic pink roses introduce a formal element. These qualities combine to create a traditional basket arrangement, appropriate for many occasions.

FOUR VARIETIES OF FOLIAGE
set the width and height of the arrangement

BEAUTIFULLY TINTED
hydrangeas add fullness and body to the finished piece

21½in (55cm)

18in (45cm)

6 mauve mop-headed hydrangeas

20 pink roses

3 stems of spray roses

10 heads of dill

10 sprigs of skimmia

10 sprigs of cherry

10 sprigs of senecio

10 sprigs of stephanandra

Basket and equipment

Block of wet florist's foam taped to plastic bowl

3½in (9cm)

8in (20cm)

Round traditional basket

5¼in (13cm)

12¾in (32cm)

44

SPRAY ROSES have attractive buds and fill in spaces around the larger roses

RED-BROWN CHERRY FOLIAGE highlights the red shades in the hydrangeas

HEADS OF DILL are kept level with the larger pink roses

DESPITE THEIR SUBTLE color, roses remain the dominant focal flower

MAKING THE BASKET

The height and width of the display are established by four types of foliage, each one filling a quarter of the base. The flowers are then added, one variety at a time, starting with the larger blooms.

KEEP LONGER SHOOTS in the center of the display

WET FLORIST'S FOAM is taped to the plastic bowl

1 Place the plastic bowl with the wet florist's foam in the basket. Cut the skimmia to varying lengths and push into the foam to fill in a quarter of the surface. Repeat with the cherry.

DARKER-COLORED CHERRY is kept to the back of the display

2 Trim the senecio and stephanandra to varying lengths. Fill in the remaining two quarters of the foam with groups of each. Use longer lengths toward the center and the sides to establish the outline of the arrangement.

EACH TYPE OF FOLIAGE fills a quarter of the surface area

Viewed from above

SET HYDRANGEA HEADS
deep into the foliage

WEAVE ROSES down
from the top to the
sides of the
arrangement

KEEP SPRAY ROSES
at a higher level
than the roses

3 Trim the hydrangea stems down to about
6in (15cm) and push them into the foam
among the foliage. Group them toward the
sides and center of the basket, keeping them deep
within the foliage.

4 Trim the roses to 8in (20cm) and group them
between the hydrangeas. Trim the lower
leaves from the spray roses. Push into the top
of the display, next to and slightly higher than the
larger roses. Finally, add the dill.

Alternative Combination

Blazing orange roses, reddish mop-headed hydrangeas,
and burnished butterfly weed change the quite formal
appearance of the basket to an exuberant, glowing,
autumnal arrangement.

Alternative flowers

RICHLY TINTED
BUTTERFLY WEED
breaks up the
larger shapes

10 sprigs
of butterfly
weed

6 reddish
mop-headed
hydrangeas

25 large
orange roses

LUSCIOUS ROSES glow
strongly as the main
focal flower

FIERY ORANGE TONES
*Hydrangeas in shades of green and red replace
the mauve variety; large-headed, open roses in
vibrant orange tones replace the pink roses; and
butterfly weed takes the place of the light green
dill. The foliage remains the same.*

Rose Basket

Echoing the flat, rounded shape of the basket arrangement on pages 44–47, this display is based on a wintry white and green theme. Random brushstrokes of white acrylic paint on the basket create a fresh, frosted effect. The flowers and foliage will last for about ten days if the florist's foam is kept moist, and wilted blooms and leaves can easily be replaced, if necessary.

LICHEN, attached with hairpin hooks, conceals the florist's foam

WHITE ROSE HEADS are simply pushed into wet florist's foam

ORNAMENTAL CABBAGE LEAVES are pushed down into the foam

ROSE LEAVES provide dark foliage to enhance the cabbage leaves and white roses

THE BASKET is lined with plastic and filled with blocks of wet florist's foam

EXTRAVAGANT VASE DISPLAY
I have clustered together an abundance of flowers by type almost to overpower a simple, dark green, glossy container.

VASE DISPLAYS

TO MY MIND there is nothing more simple or spontaneous than arranging fresh flowers in a vase. One of the most commonly attempted forms of flower arrangement, vase displays lend instant freshness and color to any setting.

A vase and its flowers should always work together, interacting to create a unified composition. Whatever its style, a display must also sit comfortably in its surroundings. Even buying carefully color-coordinated bunches of flowers, already arranged to drop into a vase, does not guarantee a successful display if you fail to consider the style and position of the container.

Flowers totally alter the look of a vessel, whether a glass vase or a wooden bowl, so choose varieties that balance well. Tall material with individual florets growing low on the stem, such as gladioli, are a natural choice for upright, tall containers, but don't be afraid to trim taller flowers, too. Lofty and majestic amaryllis, for example, when cut down take on a fuller, more luxurious appearance. Simplicity is vital for modern displays, and narrow-necked vases that keep a minimal number of stems close together and upright ensure the perfect look of cool sophistication. Provençal bowls and jugs, with their rustic associations, call for an abundance of color and texture, while flared vases need an ample amount of foliage to prevent the flowers from falling to the edge. Clear glass vases, with their relative anonymity, suit almost any setting and also allow you to make a feature of the stems.

Vase displays can last for a long time if you care for them well. Prepare the stems before starting to arrange (see pages 174–175) to keep them healthy and strong. Make sure the water is clean by replacing it every other day: stand the arrangement under running water until all the old water has been flushed out. Add flower food to the water whenever possible.

Flared Vase Display
Page 52

Cylindrical Vases
Page 54

Low Bowl Display
Page 56

Formal Country Display
Page 62

FLARED VASE DISPLAY

THE DIAMETER OF A VASE'S MOUTH will help determine the type and quantity of flowers to be used in it. This elegant flared vase calls for tall, strong, supple flowers, such as tulips, that will lend themselves to its shape while supporting one another as the stems intertwine.

MAKING THE ARRANGEMENT

Choose tulip and eucalyptus stems about twice the height of the container. Prepare all the flower and foliage stems before arranging (see page 174).

MATERIALS AND EQUIPMENT

Flowers and foliage

18in (45cm)

30 pink tulips   **15 lengths of eucalyptus**

Container

Flared glass vase

10in (25cm)

10in (25cm)

TULIP STEMS FOLLOW the line of the vase

LEAVE ONE OR TWO LEAVES on the tulip stems

STEMS have been scraped down and trimmed off neatly

ADD LENGTHS OF EUCALYPTUS between the tulips

STEMS below the water line have been stripped of leaves

1 Fill the vase three-quarters full with water. Insert between seven and ten tulips, spiraling them around the edge of the vase to follow its angle and lean over the edge.

2 Add lengths of eucalyptus between the tulip stems, making sure they lean over the vase at the same angle as the flowers.

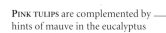

PINK TULIPS are complemented by hints of mauve in the eucalyptus

DELICATE SMALL-LEAVED EUCALYPTUS sprigs contrast with the large, smooth tulip blooms and leaves

3 Fill in the display with the remaining tulips and eucalyptus. Keep the taller stems toward the center, and angle the leaves to follow the line of the flower heads.

THICK, GREEN TULIP STEMS fill out the vase and provide light color for contrast

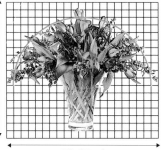

20in (50cm)

22in (55cm)

DESIGN TIP
The overall display is about twice the height of the vase, and the flowers and foliage form a dome shape above the container. The display is slightly wider than it is high.

CYLINDRICAL VASES

THE DIFFERING DIMENSIONS AND COLORS of these two cylindrical vases call for displays quite specific to each. Low, wide containers require a compact display of short, grouped flowers, while taller, narrower vases can support longer, more elegant stems and foliage on different levels. Choose flowers to highlight the texture of the container, too.

MATERIALS AND EQUIPMENT – Low Bowl

Flowers

6in (15cm)

12 red anemones **14 white anemones** **9 purple anemones**

Container

ADHESIVE TAPE GRID over the top of the bowl

Low cylindrical vase

3¼in (8cm)

6½in (16cm)

MATERIALS AND EQUIPMENT – Tall Vase

Flowers and foliage

8 lengths of eucalyptus

19⅛in (48cm)

8 stems of white amaryllis

3 shoots of globe artichoke leaves

Container

Tall cylindrical vase

8⅛in (20.5cm)

4⅛in (10.5cm)

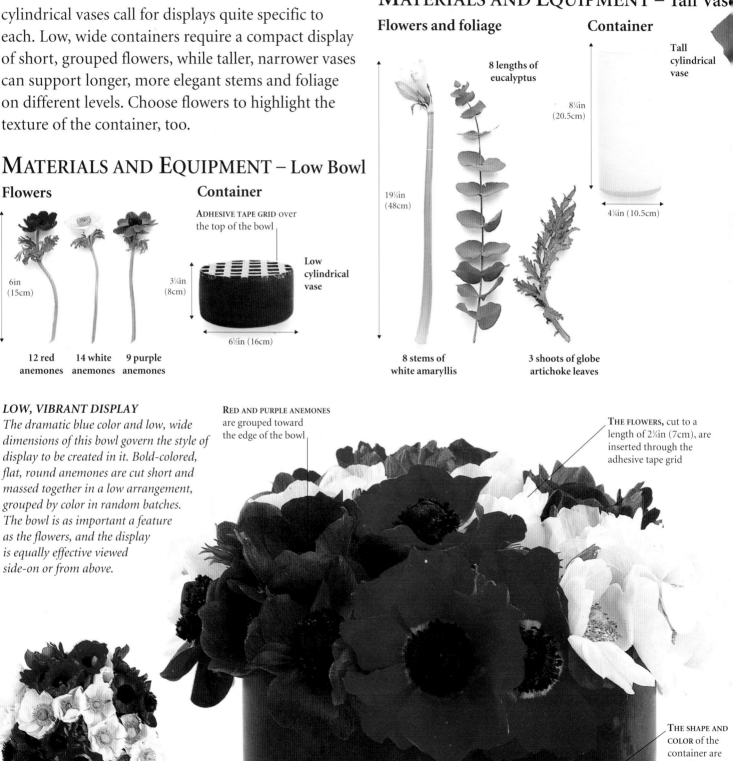

LOW, VIBRANT DISPLAY

The dramatic blue color and low, wide dimensions of this bowl govern the style of display to be created in it. Bold-colored, flat, round anemones are cut short and massed together in a low arrangement, grouped by color in random batches. The bowl is as important a feature as the flowers, and the display is equally effective viewed side-on or from above.

RED AND PURPLE ANEMONES are grouped toward the edge of the bowl

THE FLOWERS, cut to a length of 2¾in (7cm), are inserted through the adhesive tape grid

THE SHAPE AND COLOR of the container are complemented by the velvety, intense-colored anemones

Viewed from above

LONGER STEMS of amaryllis are positioned toward the back of the display

STEMS OF EUCALYPTUS fill out the display, lending height and width

GLOBE ARTICHOKE LEAVES inserted at the base of the arrangement balance the display and hang down to conceal the top of the vase

TALL, FRONT-FACING DISPLAY

Serrated silvery globe artichoke leaves juxtapose with the smooth green eucalyptus, while white amaryllis flowers dominate the display with their color and shape. The height of the vase allows flowers and foliage to extend out quite far from the sides, but the display would look equally impressive if more contained and columnlike.

FROSTED GLASS partly obscures the stems and exaggerates the silvery tones of the flowers and foliage

Side view

LOW BOWL DISPLAY

WHILE LARGE FLOWERS are usually more fitting for tall containers, they can look just as stunning in a low bowl. Here, I have cut amaryllis stems down for a display, best seen from above, that allows the viewer to appreciate the luxurious openness of the large, fleshy blooms.

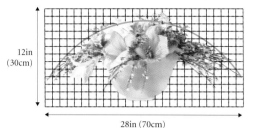

12in (30cm)

28in (70cm)

DESIGN TIP
The ingredients have been arranged low in the bowl, making the display as high as the container and twice as wide.

MATERIALS AND EQUIPMENT

Flowers and foliage

8in (20cm)

20 sprigs of broom

5 stems of peach amaryllis

5 stems of white amaryllis

8 sprigs of cineraria

Container

Low, frosted bowl

6in (15cm)

14in (35cm)

MAKING THE ARRANGEMENT

No tape grid is necessary for this display: flowers and foliage are kept compact, supporting each other.

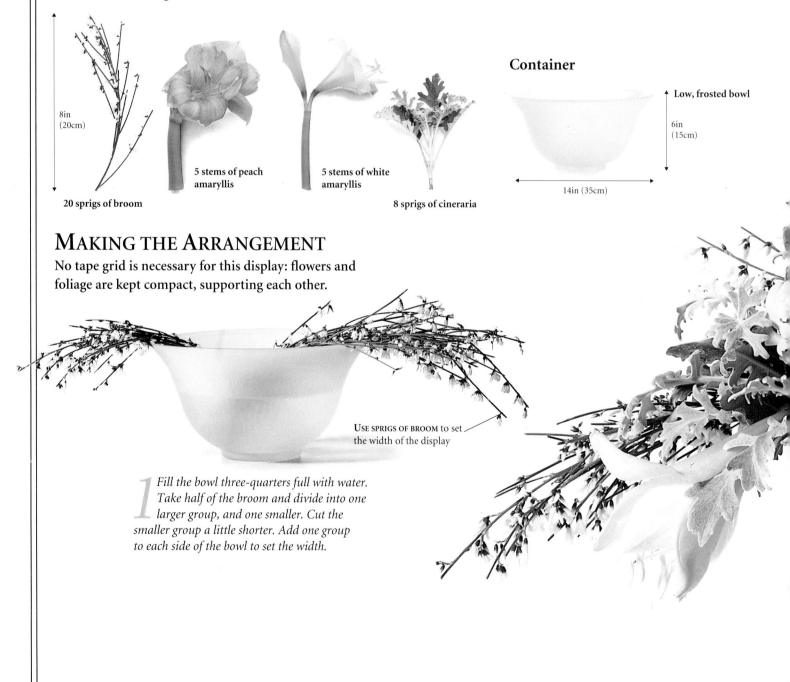

USE SPRIGS OF BROOM to set the width of the display

1 Fill the bowl three-quarters full with water. Take half of the broom and divide into one larger group, and one smaller. Cut the smaller group a little shorter. Add one group to each side of the bowl to set the width.

2 Fill the center of the bowl with amaryllis, keeping the colors separate. Place the larger flowers most centrally, with narrower heads and buds leaning over the edge of the bowl.

KEEP LARGER BLOOMS central and low

LET SMALLER FLOWERS lean over the edges of the bowl

GROUP PEACH AMARYLLIS together

Viewed from a higher angle

USE DELICATE CINERARIA to fill out the arrangement and contrast with the heavy amaryllis blooms

FROSTED GLASS CONCEALS the stems and blends with the pale flowers and foliage

3 Add sprigs of cineraria. Use them to fill out the display and hang over the bowl, subtly linking the amaryllis and broom. Add more sprigs of broom around the front and back of the bowl.

Low Rustic Bowl

A beautiful wide, low Provençal bowl has been filled with a lavish selection of fresh, summery flowers that spill out and tumble over the sides. The flamboyant abundance of the display is a result of its width and height: it is over three times the height of the bowl and twice as wide. The flowers have been arranged in the same way as those on pages 56–57, building up from the sides, but the extra width of the bowl accommodates a much taller and wider display.

SPIKY SEA HOLLY is a foil to the other soft, less rigid flowers, and echoes the blue of the bowl

LIGHT PINK FEATHERY ASTILBE contrast with the dark red snapdragons

STRONG BUT SUPPLE SNAPDRAGONS splay over the edge of the bowl, establishing the width

TRAILING TENDRILS OF JASMINE enhance the spontaneous effect and add a sweet, heady scent to the display

THE DUSKY BLUE EARTHENWARE BOWL provides a dark base for the profusion of colors in the display

VIBRANT DELPHINIUMS grouped together form the highest point of the display

SPRIGS OF SCENTED LILAC fill out one side

TINY YELLOW SPRAY ROSES are bunched around a group of larger pink roses

TRAILING FOLIAGE makes the display appear wider and balances the high delphiniums

A SINGLE LARGE HYDRANGEA LEAF, placed asymmetrically, provides structure and sets off the less substantial ivy and jasmine

59

SIMPLE MODERN VESSEL

DISPLAYS MADE IN WIDE CONTAINERS, such as this loosely arranged modern winter display, may need some extra support. I find it useful to use chicken wire, folded and curved to fill out the container, so that flower and foliage stems can be pushed in through the gaps.

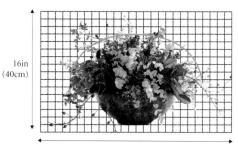

16in (40cm)

24in (60cm)

DESIGN TIP
The display mirrors the shape of the bowl, with longer lengths of foliage extending upward and from the sides to break the outline.

MATERIALS AND EQUIPMENT

Flowers and foliage

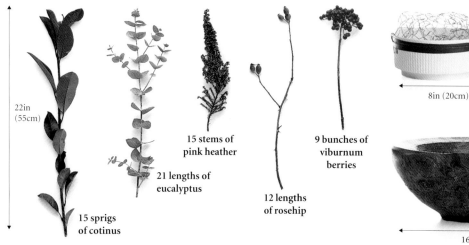

22in (55cm)

15 sprigs of cotinus

21 lengths of eucalyptus

15 stems of pink heather

12 lengths of rosehip

9 bunches of viburnum berries

Container and equipment

Plastic bowl filled with chicken wire secured with floral wires and florist's tape

4¾in (12cm)

8in (20cm)

Wooden bowl

6½in (16cm)

16in (40cm)

MAKING THE DISPLAY

Fill the plastic bowl with chicken wire, twist floral wires around the chicken wire on each side, and tape them to the outside of the bowl with florist's tape.

PUSH IN random groups of three eucalyptus lengths

1 Fill the plastic bowl three-quarters full with water and place in the wooden container. Trim the cotinus and eucalyptus to 12in (30cm) and insert into the chicken wire. Add the eucalyptus in groups of three between the cotinus.

ANGLE the stems so they point out slightly

2 *Cut the stems of heather to 8in (20cm) long. Push them into the center of the chicken wire among the cotinus and eucalyptus to form a domed shape in the center of the arrangement.*

PLACE HEATHER stems in the center of the foliage

3 *Cut the rosehips to 20in (50cm) long, and push into the plastic bowl to trail over the sides of the wooden container. Finally, push the bunches of berries deeper in the display.*

LET LENGTHS of rosehip extend farthest from the wooden bowl

PUSH IN BUNCHES of berries to fill out the display

Formal Country Display

An unusual, elegant container introduces a stylized element to a casual arrangement for a modern setting. Using chicken wire for support, as on pages 60–61, I have arranged large rounded blooms and trailing English ivy low and wide in a galvanized metal container resting on a wrought iron and wicker stand. The curved feet of the stand, sculptural lilies, and long lengths of ivy create a decorative art nouveau effect.

DELICATE HELENIUM lightens the mood with its bright color and rustic charm

ORANGE ROSES blend with the deep purples and pinks of the other flowers

THE ELEGANT LINES of the lilies promote a flowing, sinuous feel

MOP-HEADED HYDRANGEAS help shape the display with their luxurious, rounded surfaces

TRAILING IVY lends a sweeping line to the display, echoing the curves of the stand

TRAINED CHRISTMAS RING
Two ivy plants have been trained to climb around a frame and form a ring, echoing the traditional symbol of the Christmas wreath. A bow made from crimson wired French ribbon adds a festive touch and matches the coloring of the pot.

PLANTED ARRANGEMENTS

A PLANTED BOWL immediately fills me with a sense of panic. I hate with a vengeance those birdbaths with a mix of tropical-looking plants and a token African violet. They represent everything that is outdated. At last there is a new look for planted displays: gone is the plastic bowl, and in come the woven or wooden basket, and Provençal pottery. Out goes the tropical houseplant mix, and in comes the solid, one-plant variety in striking colors, potted *en masse*.

For inspiration, study the groupings of plants in gardens or woodlands. A large range of plants can be transported from the flower bed to planted containers – and from the vegetable patch and herb garden, too. If mixing species together in one display, choose plants of similar longevity and flowering times with compatible watering, heat, and light requirements.

When you choose a vessel, make sure it complements the plant not only in color but also in style. Baskets or rustic pottery are ideal counterparts to cineraria or tiny spring narcissi, which lend themselves to a country or Provençal look. Stone or metal urns overflowing with hydrangeas or orchids have a grander, more decadent aura. And even the most unassuming, drab pot can be transformed by the vibrant color and bold shape of a hyacinth with its sweet, heady scent that lingers for days. Topiary plants, trained, grown and trimmed to shape, then planted in terra-cotta pots, not only create a sense of drama in the sweeping grounds of large estates, but on a smaller scale bring character to patios, doorsteps, and windowsills of more modest homes.

Even the most understated flower or plant can be made to look really special when planted in a suitable container, and because the displays are so long-lasting, they make attractive gifts. Planted arrangements are also low on maintenance and require little practical expertise: the only skill you need to learn is how to line porous containers that have no saucer with plastic to prevent leakage. It is important, too, to choose a good potting soil.

Planted Wooden Basket
Page 66

Summer Herb Arrangement
Page 72

Potted Plant Display
Page 74

PLANTED WOODEN BASKET

A VARIATION ON THE MORE TRADITIONAL planted display, this arrangement in a wooden basket is easily assembled and makes an ideal gift. I have chosen hardy heather, crimson spray roses, and deep red pansies to complement the country basket and form a welcoming winter display. A cheerful bow made of red ribbon makes the basket appropriate for the weeks before Christmas.

MATERIALS AND EQUIPMENT

Line the wooden basket with black plastic before planting the potted flowers to prevent water from leaking out.

Plants and decoration

12¾in
(32cm)

4 pink heather plants

**3 crimson spray
rose plants**

6in
(15cm)

**3 red pansy
plants**

**5 handfuls of
bun moss**

**20in (50cm) wired French ribbon,
1in (2.5cm) wide**

Container and equipment

↑ **Painted
wooden
basket**

14in
(35cm)

13¼in(33cm)

**Black plastic,
20 x 20in (50 x 50cm)**

**Broken terra-cotta
pieces (crocks)**

**5lb (2.5kg) bag
of potting soil**

Planted Wooden Basket

A ROW OF PINK HEATHER sets
the height of the display

THE FINISHED EFFECT
*Pink heather and deep crimson spray roses
are set off by a small group of pansies in one
corner of the basket. A red bow maintains the
opulent, rich image and introduces a vibrant,
festive feeling to the country arrangement.*

PANSIES are grouped
together in one corner

A GLEAMING
CRIMSON BOW
enhances the
festive element

Viewed from a higher angle

PLANTING THE BASKET

Place half of the soil in the lined basket before
removing the plants from their pots. Once they
are all correctly positioned in the basket, add
the rest of the soil and the bun moss.

POSITION HEATHER PLANTS SO that the flowers extend beyond the handle

LINE THE BASKET with black plastic to protect it from moisture in the soil

*1 Line the basket with the square of black
plastic so that it hangs over the sides.
Strew the terra-cotta crocks evenly over
the base, and then add half the potting soil
and firm it down.*

*2 Carefully remove the heather plants
from their pots and place them in a line
across the back of the basket, so that
they stand taller than the handle. Angle the
plants on the outer edges slightly over the rim.*

PLACE SPRAY ROSES in front of the heather

*3 Remove the spray roses from their pots
and place in front of the heather plants.
Position them in a line, starting at the
left side of the basket, and leave some space in
the right-hand corner.*

GROUP PANSIES in the right-hand corner

ADD BUN MOSS to conceal the soil

4 Remove the pansies from their pot, and group them in the front right-hand corner of the basket, next to the spray roses. Add the rest of the soil around the plants, up to 1in (2.5cm) below the rim of the basket.

5 Trim off the black plastic to just below the inner rim of the basket, slightly above soil level, and add bun moss around the base of the plants. Finally, tie a bow around the handle with the wired ribbon.

Alternative Combination

Change the single-color theme to a mixed theme, using the same type of flowers, but in different colors. Keep the same ribbon to link in with the heathers retained in the back of the basket.

Alternative flowers

3 white spray rose plants

3 purple and white pansy plants

WHITE SPRAY ROSES replace the crimson variety

FRESH WINTER BASKET
Introducing white spray roses and purple and white pansies breaks up the uniformity of the display and lightens the emphasis. The overall display is brighter and fresher.

Planted Spring Bulbs

Narcissi, scillas, and other bulbs potted in interesting containers, such as these rough-hewn wooden fruit baskets, form delightful, long-lasting decorations that bring the first scents of spring indoors. Choose flowers with unopened buds, and line the baskets with plastic before potting. The arrangements will last up to two weeks if kept moist and cool, and they make charming gifts for Easter or birthdays.

THE DIFFERING LENGTHS of flower stems on each bulb break up the uniformity

TALLER SCILLAS are planted near the center

SMALL PEBBLES AND LICHEN conceal the soil and bulbs

THE GREEN-STAINED FRUIT BASKET provides color contrast with the light lichen and complements the delicate scillas

NARCISSI are planted irregularly with roughly the same amount of soil surrounding each bulb

THIN TWIGS are used to form a decorative fence around the arrangement

THE RAFFIA used to bind the twig fence adds to the rustic look

BUN MOSS is pressed between the bulbs to conceal the soil

THE SIMPLE UNPAINTED BASKET complements the twigs and yellow narcissi

SUMMER HERB ARRANGEMENT

THE DECORATIVE USE OF HERBS need not be limited to the herb garden outdoors. Here, I have potted different herbs in old terra-cotta pots, disguising the soil with moss, and grouped them together to form a kitchen window display. Similar herbs planted in an unusual low container form a long-lasting, aromatic composition.

SINGLE POTTED HERBS
When potting herbs individually, choose varieties that look quite different (allowing for culinary needs if you must). Grouped together, they form an eye-catching arrangement.

THE CURRY PLANT, with its delicate, silvery fronds, introduces a cool, pale color

TALL, NARROW STEMS of hyssop contrast with the single, fuller sage plant

BROAD-LEAVED PURPLE SAGE is a familiar culinary herb suited to a simple kitchen arrangement

Summer Herb Arrangement

STRAIGHT, SUPPLE OREGANO plants provide height at the back of the display

TALL HYSSOP SHOOTS add color to the top of the display

INDOOR HERB GARDEN
Herbs have been chosen for their contrasting shapes, textures, and colors to create a large potted arrangement. Taller plants are kept toward the back of the display, while shorter, bushy herbs fill out the center and front.

PURPLE-LEAVED SAGE is used as the middle-level herb in the center of the arrangement

ROSEMARY trails over the front, adding movement and balance

POTTED PLANT DISPLAY

SIMPLE PLANTED ARRANGEMENTS of one type of plant make appealing decorations that are very easy to maintain. Here, I have grouped two color-coordinated potted containers to form a homey composition that displays the bold colors of the flowers well.

MATERIALS AND EQUIPMENT

Choose plants that complement the color and shape of the containers. Make sure they are of similar height, at the same stage of development, and have flowers with a long life span.

Plants and moss

14in (35cm)

1 large primrose plant

5 small primrose plants

10 pieces of sheet moss

Containers and equipment

6in (15cm)

14in (35cm)

6in (15cm)

1 large, wide container and 1 cylindrical pot with a saucer

Black plastic, 20 x 20in (50 x 50cm)

Broken terra-cotta pieces (crocks)

5lb (2.5kg) bag of potting soil

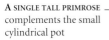

A SINGLE TALL PRIMROSE complements the small cylindrical pot

THE MAUVE CONTAINER clashes delightfully with the deep red primrose

74

POTTING THE PLANTS

*Line the container without a saucer with black
plastic, so that it hangs 2in (5cm) over the edge.
Scatter crocks over the base of both containers, and
add some soil. Remove the plants from their pots and
place in the containers, filling soil around them up to
1in (2.5cm) from the top of the pot. Firm the soil,
water well, and trim the black plastic to just
above the soil level. Add moss to conceal the soil.*

PRIMROSE HEADS
echo the color of
the container

FIRST LINE THE LARGE CONTAINER
with black plastic to prevent
water from seeping out

SOME PLANTS lean slightly
toward the edge

SHEET MOSS conceals the soil and
accentuates the unaffected charm

THE FINISHED EFFECT

*Intense clashing red and purple primroses
have been chosen to correspond with the
colors of the containers, and the light green
ribbing on the smaller pot is picked up by the
veins in the leaves.*

CASCADING URN
Flamboyant foliage and vibrant flowers cascade over a classical urn, creating an opulent, dramatic spectacle.

LARGE-SCALE ARRANGEMENTS

FEW OF US ARE FORTUNATE ENOUGH to have inherited a large family mansion, with a vast hallway that requires a huge fresh flower arrangement every week of the year. For most people a large arrangement is called for only on special occasions – religious celebrations, Christmas, Thanksgiving, weddings, and christenings or perhaps a party, birthday, anniversary, or business conference. These occasions demand large, eye-catching displays of flowers, and bold statements and extravagant effects are the order of the day.

Mantelpiece Arrangement
Page 78

I believe that a large-scale arrangement needs a little more attention to theme than a smaller, everyday display. Simply increasing the quantity of smaller flowers often leads to an undefined mass of color that fails to engage or excite the viewer. The choice of vessel can alter this immediately. An urn or pedestal creates instant drama and classical grace. A mantelpiece structure allows foliage and flowers to tumble and curl around its framework. Swags or garlands require no extra trimmings. Hung in a prominent position, they enliven even the most somber of spaces.

Making full use of accessories in a large display helps dictate the tenor of an occasion. Voluptuous twists and drapes of deep red velvet bring warmth to winter or Christmas arrangements. Fruit and vegetables used in an innovative way reflect the season and can also add a touch of humor to a display, while enhancing the shape and texture of the flowers.

Pedestal Display
Page 82

When planning a large-scale arrangement, do make sure there is ample space for it. Forcing a display into a tight area immediately dampens its impact and creates a crowded atmosphere. Choose larger flowers where possible, and group them together to form bold blocks of color. If roses or even smaller flowers are required, it is easy for them to become lost, so mass them together to ensure that they can be noticed from far away.

Long Table Decoration
Page 86

MANTELPIECE ARRANGEMENT

THE SOBER ELEGANCE and straight lines of a mantelpiece often demand a formal flower display, but here, to create a freer, more spontaneous effect, I have combined informal potted plants, foliage, and moss in a relaxed, abundant arrangement that covers the entire mantelpiece. The dark mauve ornamental cabbages, heather, and pansies lend depth to the display.

DEEP PINK HEATHER softens the arrangement and lends height

THE FINISHED EFFECT
A rich combination of textures and surprising lack of symmetry in the arrangement produce a naturally impromptu display.

OPEN, ROUNDED ornamental cabbages are instantly eye-catching

RED PANSIES provide tiny pools of color

TRAILING IVY counterbalances the height of the arrangement and adds fluid lines

MATERIALS AND EQUIPMENT

A layer of black plastic protects the mantelpiece and is hidden with clumps of moss and trailing English ivy.

Equipment

Black plastic,
8in x 4ft (20cm x 1.2m)

12 floral wires,
10½in (26cm) long, 71 gauge

Plants and moss

12in
(30cm)

3 variegated
English ivy
plants

2 purple
ornamental cabbages

2 pink
heather plants

5 red
pansy plants

12 handfuls of
bun moss

12 handfuls of
sphagnum moss

CLUMPS OF MOSS conceal the
black plastic and plant pots

MAKING THE ARRANGEMENT

Potted plants are placed at different angles and arranged asymmetrically along the mantelpiece. Clumps of moss conceal the pots and the gaps between them.

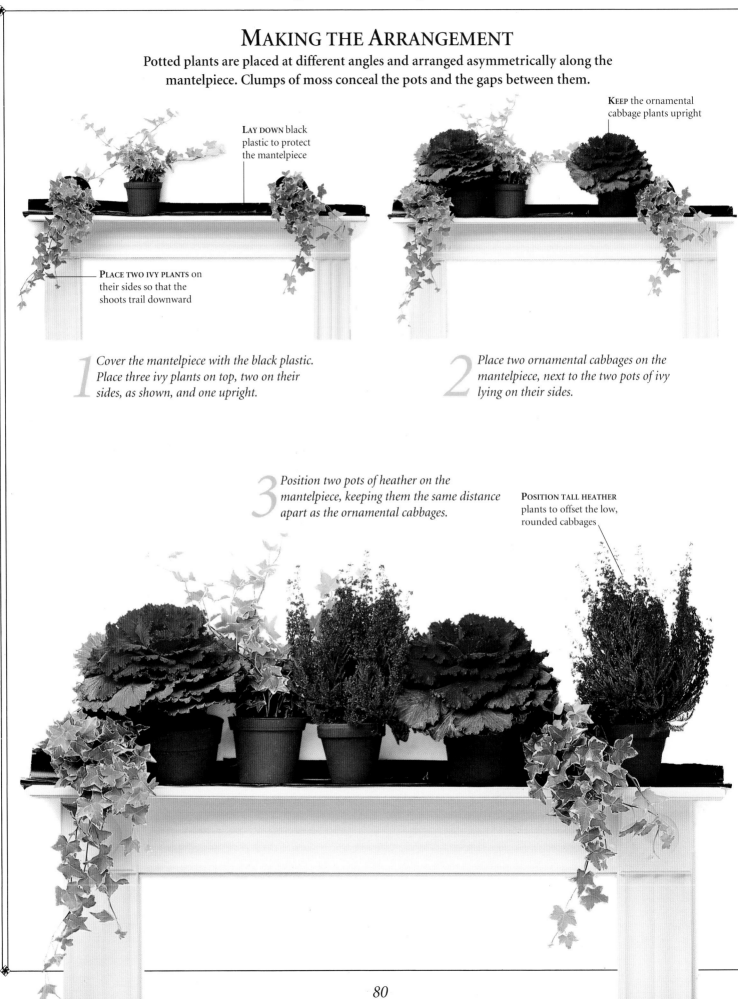

LAY DOWN black plastic to protect the mantelpiece

KEEP the ornamental cabbage plants upright

PLACE TWO IVY PLANTS on their sides so that the shoots trail downward

1 Cover the mantelpiece with the black plastic. Place three ivy plants on top, two on their sides, as shown, and one upright.

2 Place two ornamental cabbages on the mantelpiece, next to the two pots of ivy lying on their sides.

3 Position two pots of heather on the mantelpiece, keeping them the same distance apart as the ornamental cabbages.

POSITION TALL HEATHER plants to offset the low, rounded cabbages

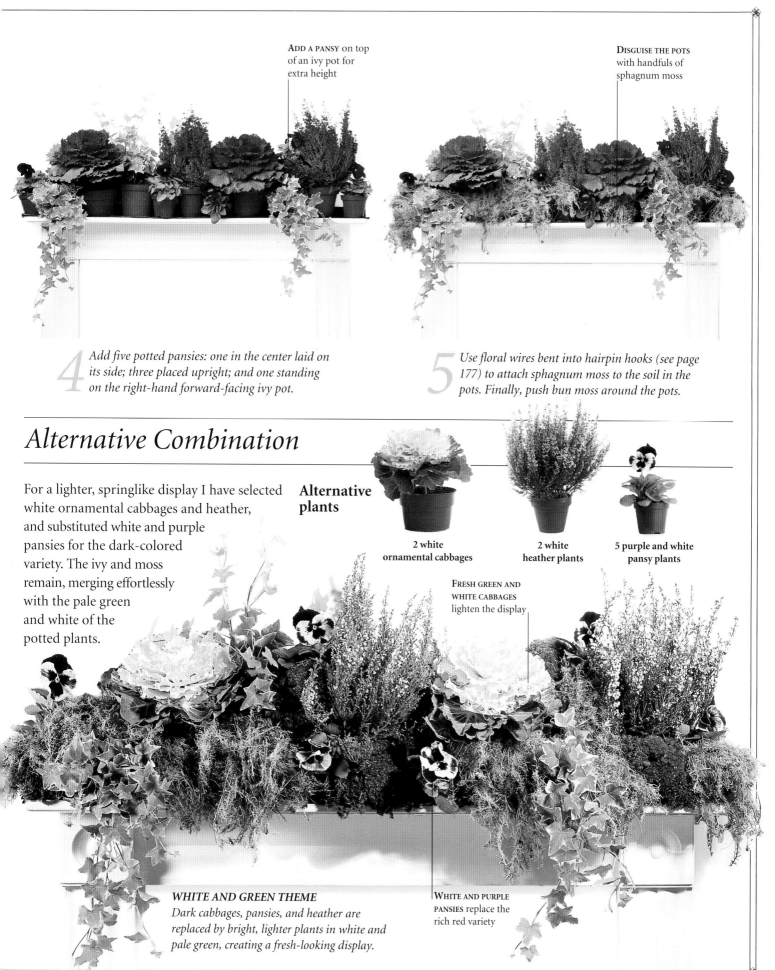

ADD A PANSY on top of an ivy pot for extra height

DISGUISE THE POTS with handfuls of sphagnum moss

4 *Add five potted pansies: one in the center laid on its side; three placed upright; and one standing on the right-hand forward-facing ivy pot.*

5 *Use floral wires bent into hairpin hooks (see page 177) to attach sphagnum moss to the soil in the pots. Finally, push bun moss around the pots.*

Alternative Combination

For a lighter, springlike display I have selected white ornamental cabbages and heather, and substituted white and purple pansies for the dark-colored variety. The ivy and moss remain, merging effortlessly with the pale green and white of the potted plants.

Alternative plants

2 white ornamental cabbages

2 white heather plants

5 purple and white pansy plants

FRESH GREEN AND WHITE CABBAGES lighten the display

WHITE AND GREEN THEME
Dark cabbages, pansies, and heather are replaced by bright, lighter plants in white and pale green, creating a fresh-looking display.

WHITE AND PURPLE PANSIES replace the rich red variety

PEDESTAL DISPLAY

AN OPULENT PEDESTAL DISPLAY brings splendor and high drama to a large space, such as a hall or dining room. Make sure the pedestal stand and the arrangement merge comfortably: here I have used raffia to trail down the column, helping to integrate it with the main arrangement, but fabric or long lengths of foliage also work well.

MATERIALS AND EQUIPMENT

Flowers and foliage are built up on blocks of wet foam surrounded by chicken wire and taped to a wide, low bowl.

6½ft (2m)

3¼ft (1m)

DESIGN TIP
The display is as high as the pedestal and twice as wide. The ingredients are placed asymmetrically and a large bunch of raffia trails down one side, forming a bond between the flowers and the column to balance the display visually.

Flowers, foliage, and decoration

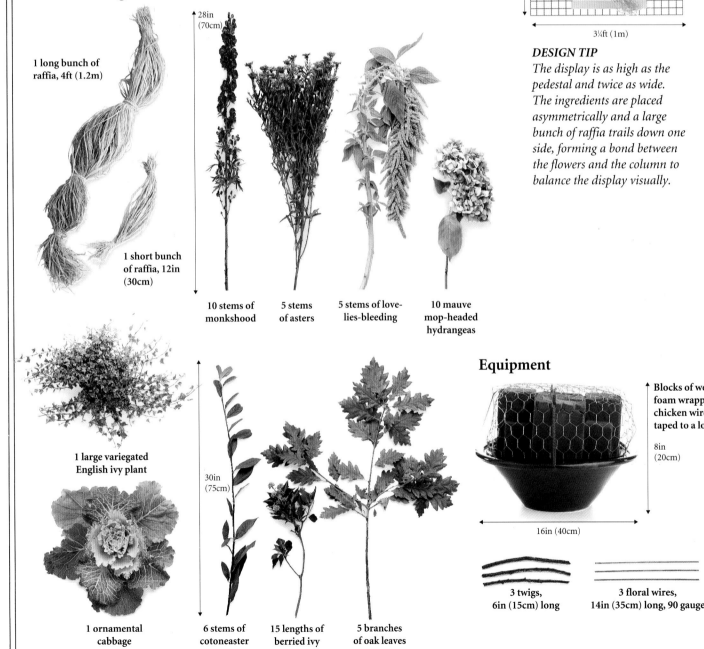

1 long bunch of raffia, 4ft (1.2m)

28in (70cm)

1 short bunch of raffia, 12in (30cm)

10 stems of monkshood

5 stems of asters

5 stems of love-lies-bleeding

10 mauve mop-headed hydrangeas

1 large variegated English ivy plant

1 ornamental cabbage

30in (75cm)

6 stems of cotoneaster

15 lengths of berried ivy

5 branches of oak leaves

Equipment

Blocks of wet florist's foam wrapped in chicken wire and taped to a low bowl

8in (20cm)

16in (40cm)

3 twigs, 6in (15cm) long

3 floral wires, 14in (35cm) long, 90 gauge

THE FINISHED EFFECT
Natural raffia and an ornamental cabbage immediately catch the eye and add an element of rustic simplicity to counteract the grand associations of the pedestal style.

A SMALL BUNCH of raffia continues the line of the longer trailing raffia tail

FLOWERS AND IVY break up the triangular outline created by the lengths of foliage

MOP-HEADED HYDRANGEAS are pushed deep into the display

DROOPING LOVE-LIES-BLEEDING gracefully leads the eye from the arrangement down the column

MAKING THE PEDESTAL DISPLAY

Both bunches of raffia are attached with
floral wires twisted into double leg mounts
(see page 177); all other ingredients are
simply pushed into the wet florist's foam.

PUSH IN the foliage
at slightly different
lengths within
each group

*1 Place the bowl on the pedestal and attach
the large bunch of raffia to the front right-
hand corner of the foam. Cut the cabbage
stem on a slant and push into the top right-hand
corner. Push the twigs into the drainage holes in
the ivy pot and press in by the cabbage.*

HOOK ON
the large
raffia bunch
with double
leg mounts

*2 Push the lengths of cotoneaster into the
center of the back of the foam to form
the highest point of the display. Push
the berried ivy into the upper left side, and
the oak leaves into the lower right side.*

FAN OUT the monkshood
to fill in the triangular
outline

*3 Add the stems of monkshood to the
right of the cotoneaster, slightly lower
and fanning out down the side. Divide
the asters into two groups. Push one group
into the foam to the left of the ivy, angled
downward, and add the other to the right
of the cabbage.*

SET THE WIDTH of
the left side of the
display with asters

STEMS of love-lies-bleeding add a sense of asymmetry

PUSH IN STEMS of love-lies-bleeding to complement the raffia and conceal part of the pedestal

4 *Divide the love-lies-bleeding into two groups. Push one group into the foam to the right of the raffia, and add the other stems to the left of the ivy plant. Finally, push the hydrangeas deep into the arrangement and attach the shorter bunch of raffia with a double leg mount to the center of the display, angled to continue the line of the longer length of raffia.*

Side view

LONG TABLE DECORATION

DESIGNED TO LIE ALONG THE CENTER of a dining table, this fresh, informal centerpiece evokes a sense of eating alfresco indoors and can be made to fit any table. I have combined earthy moss and bark with delicate yellow flowers and foliage to create a decorative band that is reminiscent of a woodland floor or a spring flower bed. The tallest flowers on the top of the centerpiece are as long as the lengths of bark on the sides, creating a visually and structurally balanced band.

12in (30cm)

4ft (1.2m)

DESIGN TIP
The finished band can be bent to form a curved centerpiece for a table surface.

THE FINISHED EFFECT
Spring flowers and foliage are arranged in groups to look as if they are growing naturally out of the moss. English ivy is added between the other material and appears to be growing from side to side along the band, reinforcing the natural look.

PLANTS ARE GROUPED by type, then placed at different heights and levels

ROSES AND ANGELICA are cut down short

PIECES OF BARK jut out from the arrangement

86

MATERIALS AND EQUIPMENT

You will need some black plastic to cover the base of the band – this is to protect the tabletop from the moisture in the florist's foam.

Flowers and foliage

10in (25cm)

40 sprigs of broom (1 large branch)

25 narcissi

20 stems of achillea

10 stems of yellow spray roses

20 stems of mimosa

6in (15cm)

25 sprigs of ivy

10 sprigs of angelica

6 handfuls of sheet moss

15 pieces of bark, some moss-covered

Equipment

Chicken wire, 12 x 36in (30 x 90cm)

2 blocks of wet florist's foam

10 handfuls of sphagnum moss

30 floral wires, 14in (35cm) long, 90 gauge

Black plastic, 6in x 3½ft (15cm x 1m)

IVY SPRIGS alternate from side to side, weaving along the band

MAKING THE DECORATION

The base is made by enclosing blocks of wet florist's foam in chicken wire. Handfuls of moss between the foam blocks act as hinges, making the band flexible.

CUT OFF THE CHICKEN WIRE
2in (5cm) from the ends
of the foam

ATTACH BLACK PLASTIC to
protect the table surface from
the wet florist's foam

CUT FLORAL WIRES in
half and bend into
hairpin hooks

1 Cut two blocks of soaked florist's foam into three sections each and place along the center of the chicken wire, leaving a gap of 2in (5cm) between each block. Fill the gaps with handfuls of sphagnum moss.

2 Wrap the chicken wire around the foam and sew the sides together with floral wires. Fold the chicken wire around the end of the band like a package and push the ends back into the foam.

3 Place the black plastic over the band, wrapping it 1in (2.5cm) over the sides. Attach it to the base by pushing floral wires bent into hairpin hooks (see page 177) through the plastic into the foam.

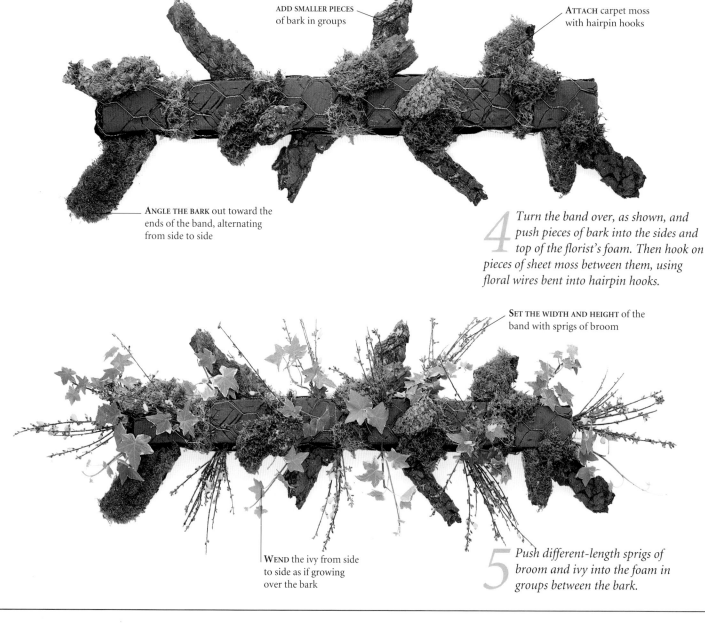

ADD SMALLER PIECES
of bark in groups

ATTACH carpet moss
with hairpin hooks

ANGLE THE BARK out toward the
ends of the band, alternating
from side to side

4 Turn the band over, as shown, and push pieces of bark into the sides and top of the florist's foam. Then hook on pieces of sheet moss between them, using floral wires bent into hairpin hooks.

SET THE WIDTH AND HEIGHT of the
band with sprigs of broom

WEND the ivy from side
to side as if growing
over the bark

5 Push different-length sprigs of broom and ivy into the foam in groups between the bark.

PUSH LARGER HEADS deeper into the foam

6 Add the narcissi and mimosa in random groups, weaving them along the top of the band and from side to side.

ANGLE FLOWER HEADS to point in different directions

7 Add the roses and mimosa in the same way, pushing them in to sit at different heights along the band.

ADD MORE IVY to fill in any gaps

8 Fill in any gaps with more ivy. Finally, add groups of angelica on top of the band, pushing them low into the foam.

FRESH FLOWERS FOR SPECIAL OCCASIONS

No festivity is complete without the natural beauty of fresh flowers. Their uplifting colors and fragrances make them the essential finishing touch. When choosing flowers for special events, consider color and form very carefully. Flamboyant blooms, such as sculptural lilies, immediately convey extravagance, while other flowers, such as romantic roses, have symbolic associations that may suit them to a particular occasion.

SIMPLE TIED POSY

THE TIED POSY, or hostess bouquet as it is sometimes known, has, I am pleased to say, gained in popularity over the traditional flat bouquet, and is a wonderful gift to give and receive. Flowers and foliage are spirally bound (see page 176) and the stems trimmed to one length, making the posy freestanding. It arrives ready to be placed in a vase, with no further arranging necessary by the recipient.

PALE GREEN EUCALYPTUS LEAVES break out from the dome shape, striking a note of informality

MAKING THE POSY
Spiral flowers and foliage, binding every three or four stems with string (see page 176) to create an evenly domed shape and a neat waist that is later bound with ribbon. The binding point on each stem should be 8in (20cm) from the top of the flower, making a posy 16in (40cm) wide.

PURPLE LISIANTHUS has a delicacy that sets the tone of the display

SHINY RED ROSEHIPS add textural contrast and lift the muted green of the foliage

THISTLELIKE CARDOONS introduce a rougher surface to vie with the delicate flowers

Viewed from above

A SELECTION OF POSIES

WHEN MAKING SIMPLE TIED POSIES, make sure the effect is even and dome-shaped as you work, and that the stems are securely bound (see page 176) so that the finished posy is freestanding. The distance between the top of the flower and the binding point should be the same for each stem, making the posy twice as wide as this length.

INFORMAL MODERN POSY
The influence of contemporary fashion and style trends extends to flower arranging, and this posy gains its young, modern feel from the bold, bright, simple ingredients. Sunflowers, a favorite at the florist's, contrast with soft, supple timothy, variegated privet, and strong, well-defined hosta leaves.

Viewed from above

VIBRANT SUNFLOWERS immediately catch the eye, giving the posy a sense of warmth and spontaneity

SUPPLE, FEATHERY TIMOTHY softens the effect of the hosta leaves and contrasts with the sunflowers

ALCHEMILLA provides a fresh, acid lime color and flowing line

COUNTRY POSY

For a casual, informal posy, I have combined several small-scale flowers and foliage in whites, purples, and greens. No one color predominates and there are few distinct shapes. The binding, made of braided raffia, complements this bountiful, natural bouquet.

Viewed from above

HYPERICUM BERRIES contribute depth and deep color

STEMS are spirally bound and tied with a raffia braid

SHINY RIBBON echoes the two-tone roses

CLASSIC FORMAL POSY

For a more formal special occasion, choose sophisticated flowers and rich binding ribbon, keeping ingredients simple, but select. Here, a classic rose dominates the traditional small posy, intermingled with mint and hypericum berries.

HINTS OF MAUVE in the mint complement the roses

95

BOUTONNIERES

WHILE BOUTONNIERES are particularly appropriate for special occasions such as weddings and seasonal celebrations, they can be worn to adorn everyday clothing, too. Choose blooms and foliage in prime condition, then wire and bind them together as near to the time of use as possible. Boutonnieres will last for one day.

THREE SEA HOLLY LEAVES
support a central head

MAKING BOUTONNIERES

Wire and bind the leaves and flowers individually (see pages 178–180), then bind them parallel to each other, one at a time, to avoid messy knots and twists of wire.

LARGER THREE-LEAFED SPRIG
acts as the back support

1 Individually wire two single rose leaves and one three-leafed sprig with fine floral wires (see page 178). Bind the wire stems with fine florist's tape (see page 180).

2 Wire the rose bud (see page 178) and bind the wire stems with tape, as before. Lay the rose against the three-leafed sprig and bind the two together with tape.

3 Bind the two single leaves one at a time to the front of the rose and the three-leafed sprig. Bend the wired leaves into shape and adjust the angle of the rose head if necessary.

SEA HOLLY
This simple boutonniere made from three sea holly leaves and one flower head makes an original, stylish decoration that can be worn with practically anything on any occasion.

SINGLE GARDENIA BLOOM
supported by three dark green, glossy leaves

FINE WIRE has been passed through the rose head and a heavier-gauge wire pushed up into the base

USE FINE FLORIST'S TAPE
to bind the wired stems together

GARDENIA
For a classic boutonniere that makes a very special alternative to the usual carnation, try a single creamy gardenia against three leaves.

TULIPS

Two extravagant tulips and two leaves have been wired and bound together with fine florist's tape. This is concealed by natural-colored string. Casual and spontaneous, this type of artless boutonniere looks fresh and stylish.

NATURAL STRING effectively conceals the fine tape, binding the flowers and leaves at one point

TULIP FLOWER STEMS have been wired internally for support, so the wires do not show

LAUREL LEAF acts as the backdrop and support

FLOWERS AND LEAVES have been simply bound at one point, leaving bare stems exposed

LILY-OF-THE-VALLEY

Four stems of lily-of-the-valley have been wired and bound to three laurel leaves. Note that the stems have not been individually bound with fine florist's tape – they are bound together at one point only.

ONE CINERARIA LEAF points downward, concealing the bound stems

A SINGLE IVY LEAF is attached to one side of the gerbera

MIXED FOLIAGE

Create a highly effective boutonniere without flowers by using a selection of unusual foliage. Here, trailing berried laurel adorns a cluster of cineraria, holly, ivy, and laurel leaves.

BERRIED LAUREL trails down from the boutonniere

GERBERA AND IVY

A single, deep crimson gerbera is backed by a large, variegated ivy leaf. Such a bold, simple boutonniere forms an immediate, eye-catching "brooch."

97

MIDSUMMER HEADDRESS

I HAVE CHOSEN DELICATE, SWEET-SCENTED FLOWERS in shades of purple and pink to adorn this romantic, traditional headdress, ideal for a summer wedding. Individually wired and bound flowers and foliage are attached to the main band with fine florist's tape. The main band is made of two long floral wires, also bound with fine florist's tape, about 2in (5cm) longer than the circumference of the wearer's head.

MATERIALS AND EQUIPMENT

Headdresses should be kept light, so you should remove stems and excess foliage and choose fine floral wires and fine florist's tape.

Flowers and foliage

25 single variegated ivy leaves

6 sprigs of purple lilac

6 purple freesias

6 pink roses

6 heads of viburnum

Equipment

2 floral wires, 14in (35cm) long, 90 gauge

60 floral wires, 6in (15cm) long, 30 gauge

Roll of fine florist's tape

VARIEGATED IVY LEAVES weave through the flowers from side to side

DEEPLY SCENTED LILAC and roses are perfect flowers for a headdress

ANGLE THE FLOWER HEADS to alternate from side to side

MAKING THE HEADDRESS

Wire and bind all the flowers and foliage (see pages 178–180) before starting to work.

1 For the main band, overlap the 90-gauge floral wires by ¾in (2cm) and bind them together with tape. Starting 1in (2.5cm) from one end, bind two wired ivy leaves to the left side with the tape. Attach a wired lilac sprig to the other side, then an ivy leaf. Add a freesia to the left side, and a rose to the right. Add an ivy leaf and a viburnum head to the left.

ADD THE SAME NUMBER of leaves and flowers in each of the six sections

THE MAIN BAND is made by binding two long stub wires together

THE FINISHED EFFECT

The alternating angles of the flowers and ivy ensure the even distribution of color and shapes along the band. The headdress can be made one day in advance. Keep it fresh by spraying with water and covering with damp tissue paper in a cool place.

LIME GREEN VIBURNUM contrasts with the ivy and complements the light pink roses

SPLIT THE TAPE down its length to make it narrower and lighter

THE SEQUENCE REPEATS on each side of the band, starting with two ivy leaves

Viewed from the back

Side view

2 Beginning on the right side, add two ivy leaves, then the wired flowers and ivy in the same order as step 1. Repeat a further four times, starting each sequence on a different side from the previous one. Finally, bend the band around the head and twist the ends together.

SHOWER BOUQUET

A WEDDING BOUQUET is probably one of the most intricate and time-consuming arrangements you will ever make. This breathtaking bouquet is quite complicated to construct, and you should attempt the project only after you have completely mastered the techniques of wiring flowers individually and in units (see pages 177–181). Your effort will be well rewarded.

24in
(60cm)

12in (30cm)

DESIGN TIP
The bouquet forms two triangles, one pointing up, the other, twice as long, pointing down. The "return," the top part of the bouquet, forms the upper triangle, and the trail forms the longer lower triangle.

MATERIALS AND EQUIPMENT
Blooms must be absolutely fresh – remove flowers and foliage directly from potted plants, if possible.

Flowers and foliage

18in
(45cm)

1 stephanotis plant

12in
(30cm)

10 lily-of-the-valley leaves and 22 flowers

5 sprigs of gardenia (blooms, buds, leaves)

10 lengths of assorted plain and variegated ivy

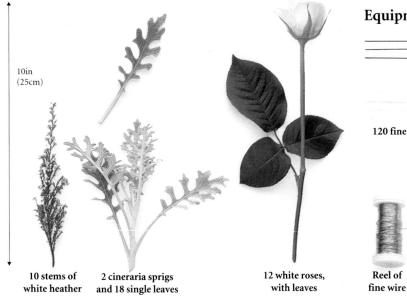

10in
(25cm)

10 stems of white heather

2 cineraria sprigs and 18 single leaves

12 white roses, with leaves

Equipment

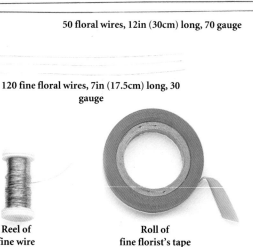

50 floral wires, 12in (30cm) long, 70 gauge

120 fine floral wires, 7in (17.5cm) long, 30 gauge

Reel of fine wire

Roll of fine florist's tape

6½ft (2m) satin ribbon, 1in (2.5cm) wide

THE FINISHED EFFECT
The color combination is limited to whites, creams, and greens, creating a traditional, delicate impression that would complement a wide variety of wedding dresses.

VOLUPTUOUS, creamy roses create a romantic mood

SNOWY GARDENIAS exude a deep, delicious scent

DELICATE LILY-OF-THE-VALLEY bells enhance the feminine tone

TRAILING IVY contributes to the classical associations

BOUQUET HANDLE
The covered wired stems are bound with satin ribbon (see page 183) and decorated with a double bow (see page 182).

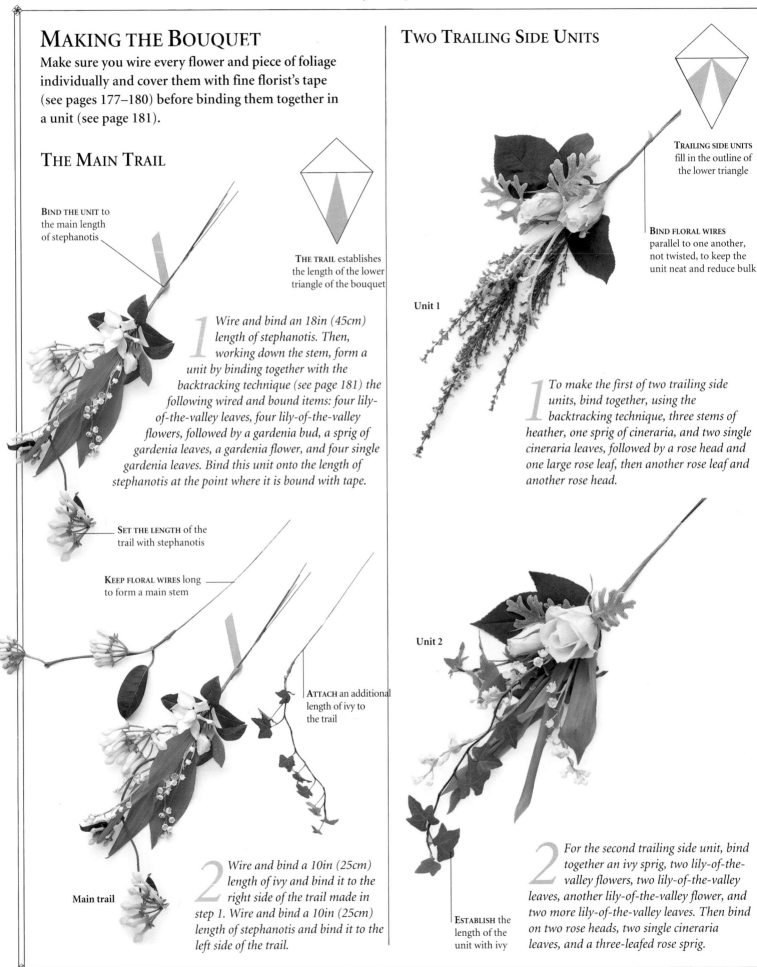

MAKING THE BOUQUET

Make sure you wire every flower and piece of foliage individually and cover them with fine florist's tape (see pages 177–180) before binding them together in a unit (see page 181).

THE MAIN TRAIL

BIND THE UNIT to the main length of stephanotis

THE TRAIL establishes the length of the lower triangle of the bouquet

1 Wire and bind an 18in (45cm) length of stephanotis. Then, working down the stem, form a unit by binding together with the backtracking technique (see page 181) the following wired and bound items: four lily-of-the-valley leaves, four lily-of-the-valley flowers, followed by a gardenia bud, a sprig of gardenia leaves, a gardenia flower, and four single gardenia leaves. Bind this unit onto the length of stephanotis at the point where it is bound with tape.

SET THE LENGTH of the trail with stephanotis

KEEP FLORAL WIRES long to form a main stem

ATTACH an additional length of ivy to the trail

Main trail

2 Wire and bind a 10in (25cm) length of ivy and bind it to the right side of the trail made in step 1. Wire and bind a 10in (25cm) length of stephanotis and bind it to the left side of the trail.

TWO TRAILING SIDE UNITS

TRAILING SIDE UNITS fill in the outline of the lower triangle

BIND FLORAL WIRES parallel to one another, not twisted, to keep the unit neat and reduce bulk

Unit 1

1 To make the first of two trailing side units, bind together, using the backtracking technique, three stems of heather, one sprig of cineraria, and two single cineraria leaves, followed by a rose head and one large rose leaf, then another rose leaf and another rose head.

Unit 2

ESTABLISH the length of the unit with ivy

2 For the second trailing side unit, bind together an ivy sprig, two lily-of-the-valley flowers, two lily-of-the-valley leaves, another lily-of-the-valley flower, and two more lily-of-the-valley leaves. Then bind on two rose heads, two single cineraria leaves, and a three-leafed rose sprig.

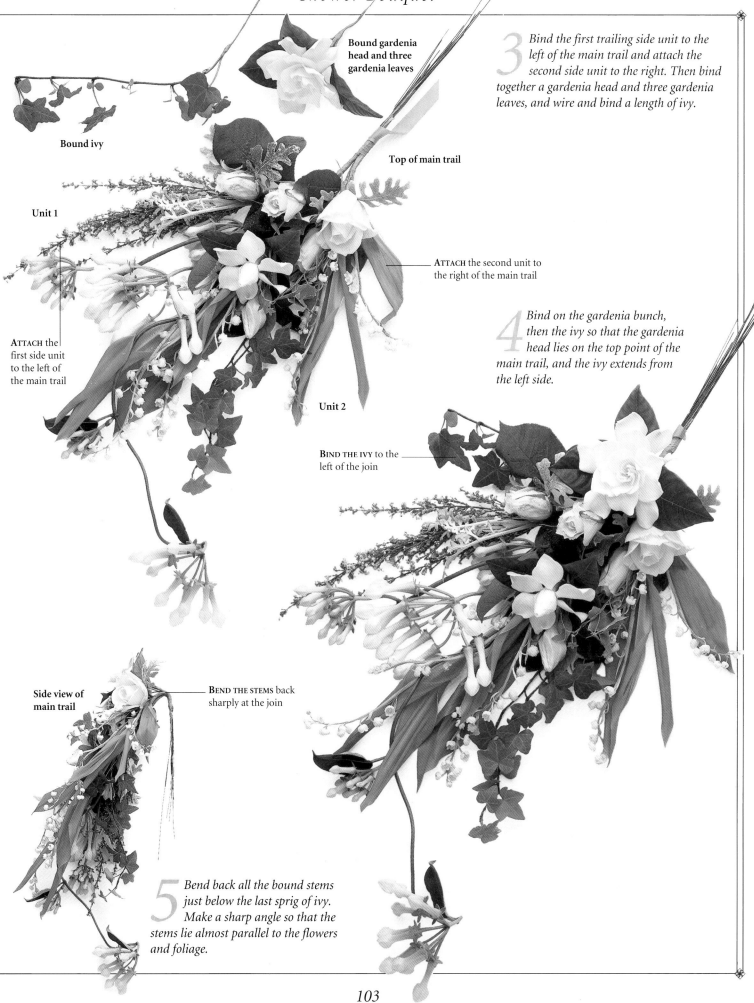

Bound gardenia
head and three
gardenia leaves

Bound ivy

Top of main trail

Unit 1

ATTACH the
first side unit
to the left of
the main trail

ATTACH the second unit to
the right of the main trail

Unit 2

BIND THE IVY to the
left of the join

Side view of
main trail

BEND THE STEMS back
sharply at the join

3 *Bind the first trailing side unit to the
left of the main trail and attach the
second side unit to the right. Then bind
together a gardenia head and three gardenia
leaves, and wire and bind a length of ivy.*

4 *Bind on the gardenia bunch,
then the ivy so that the gardenia
head lies on the top point of the
main trail, and the ivy extends from
the left side.*

5 *Bend back all the bound stems
just below the last sprig of ivy.
Make a sharp angle so that the
stems lie almost parallel to the flowers
and foliage.*

THE RETURN

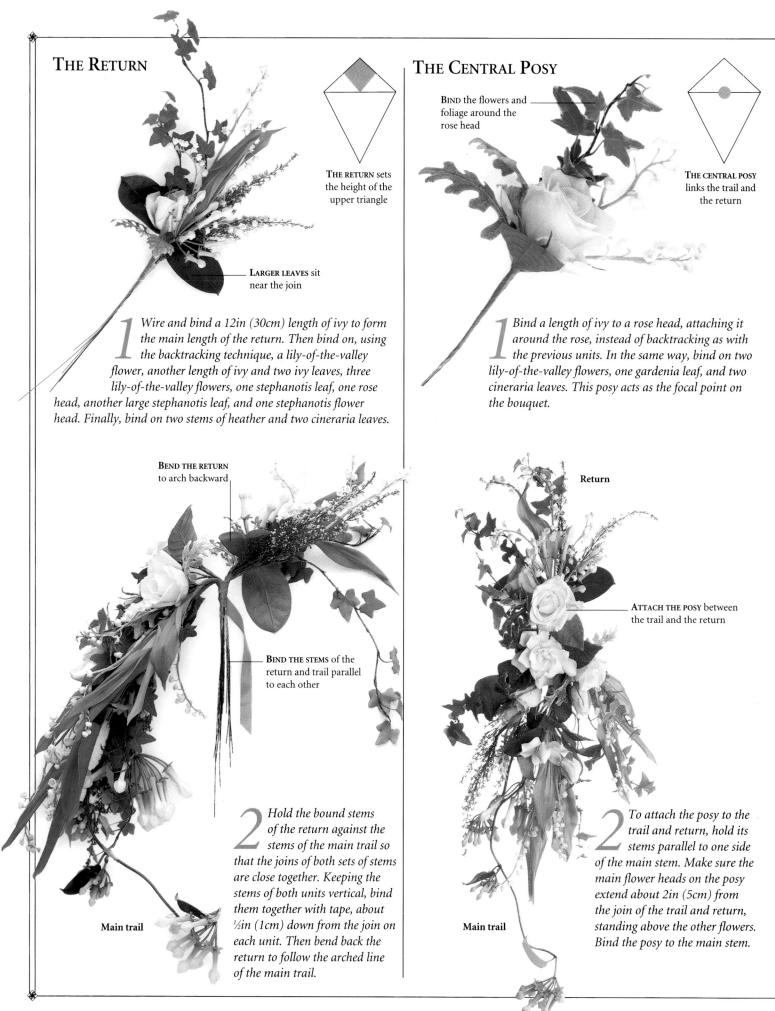

THE RETURN sets the height of the upper triangle

LARGER LEAVES sit near the join

1 Wire and bind a 12in (30cm) length of ivy to form the main length of the return. Then bind on, using the backtracking technique, a lily-of-the-valley flower, another length of ivy and two ivy leaves, three lily-of-the-valley flowers, one stephanotis leaf, one rose head, another large stephanotis leaf, and one stephanotis flower head. Finally, bind on two stems of heather and two cineraria leaves.

BEND THE RETURN to arch backward

BIND THE STEMS of the return and trail parallel to each other

Main trail

2 Hold the bound stems of the return against the stems of the main trail so that the joins of both sets of stems are close together. Keeping the stems of both units vertical, bind them together with tape, about ½in (1cm) down from the join on each unit. Then bend back the return to follow the arched line of the main trail.

THE CENTRAL POSY

BIND the flowers and foliage around the rose head

THE CENTRAL POSY links the trail and the return

1 Bind a length of ivy to a rose head, attaching it around the rose, instead of backtracking as with the previous units. In the same way, bind on two lily-of-the-valley flowers, one gardenia leaf, and two cineraria leaves. This posy acts as the focal point on the bouquet.

Return

ATTACH THE POSY between the trail and the return

Main trail

2 To attach the posy to the trail and return, hold its stems parallel to one side of the main stem. Make sure the main flower heads on the posy extend about 2in (5cm) from the join of the trail and return, standing above the other flowers. Bind the posy to the main stem.

TWO MAIN SIDE UNITS

Unit 1

Unit 2

THE SIDE UNITS set the width of the bouquet

FILLER UNITS

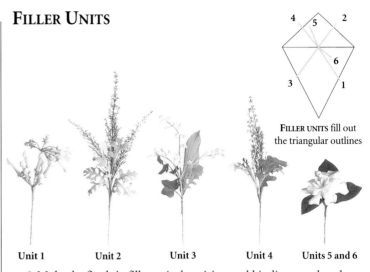

Unit 1   **Unit 2**   **Unit 3**   **Unit 4**   **Units 5 and 6**

FILLER UNITS fill out the triangular outlines

1 For the first unit, use the backtracking technique to bind three lily-of-the-valley flowers, a gardenia leaf, one stephanotis flower, and two rose heads to two lengths of ivy. Then make a second unit, the same size as the first. Bind a length of ivy to two lily-of-the-valley flowers, followed by a cineraria leaf, one rose head, one rose leaf, another rose head, a rose leaf, and finally a rose head.

1 Make the final six filler units by wiring and binding together the following elements: Unit 1: two stephanotis flower heads; Unit 2: three heather stems and six small cineraria leaves; Unit 3: one lily-of-the-valley leaf, three lily-of-the-valley flowers, two small ivy sprigs, and one cineraria leaf; Unit 4: two heather stems, one cineraria sprig and one large cineraria leaf. Make units 5 and 6 from one gardenia flower and three gardenia leaves each.

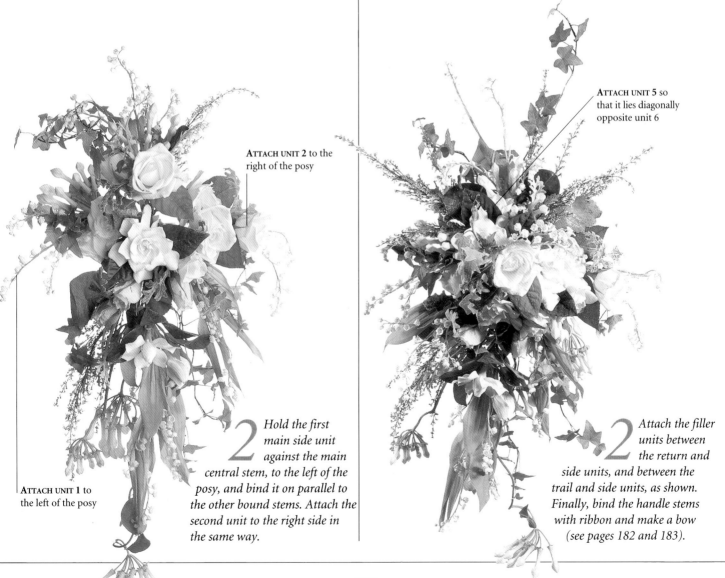

ATTACH UNIT 2 to the right of the posy

ATTACH UNIT 1 to the left of the posy

2 Hold the first main side unit against the main central stem, to the left of the posy, and bind it on parallel to the other bound stems. Attach the second unit to the right side in the same way.

ATTACH UNIT 5 so that it lies diagonally opposite unit 6

2 Attach the filler units between the return and side units, and between the trail and side units, as shown. Finally, bind the handle stems with ribbon and make a bow (see pages 182 and 183).

THANKSGIVING DISPLAY

CELEBRATE THE SEASON OF BOUNTIFUL PRODUCE with a lavish basket display that combines vegetables, flowers, and foliage. Blocks of dry foam are used to support the pumpkins, while the flowers and foliage are pushed into wet florist's foam. This keeps the vegetables grouped together on one side, with the fresh flowers and foliage on the other, following the principle of grouping ingredients by type.

PUMPKINS are kept to one side of the basket

MAKING THE DISPLAY
Use blocks of dry foam to fill out the basket on one side, then place the pumpkins on top. Tape blocks of wet florist's foam to a plastic bowl and place this in the base of the other half of the basket. Finally, push the fresh flowers and foliage into the wet florist's foam, cutting the stems on a slant.

A LARGE, RUSTIC BASKET enhances the harvest theme

SMALL, DELICATE HELENIUM
lighten the heavier shapes

MOP-HEADED HYDRANGEAS
fill out the display as
recessionary flowers

FIERY ORANGE RED HOT POKERS
pick up and enhance the
orange pumpkins

**A CRINKLED, BROWNING
LEAF** contrasts with the
brighter colors

HARVEST DECORATION

FRUIT AND FOLIAGE in the deep russets, reds, and browns of autumn are ideal for harvest arrangements. Here, a large weathered terra-cotta pot has been piled high with smaller terra-cotta pots, secured with sticks to wet florist's foam. Shiny horse chestnuts, pink heather, and cotoneaster berries fill the pots, while grapes tumble over the edge, accompanied by gleaming red apples. Trailing lengths of mature berried English ivy entwine with more pots, apples, grapes, and horse chestnuts strewn around the central pot to enhance the impression of opulence.

MAKING THE DECORATION
Line the large terra-cotta pot with black plastic and fill with blocks of wet florist's foam. Angle the smaller pots to face in different directions, and secure them to the foam with sticks pushed through their drainage holes.

SMALL POTS are secured with sticks pushed through their base into the foam

LENGTHS OF BERRIED COTONEASTER lean out, linking the main pot with the materials lying around it

IVY extends the width of the display and continues the impression of ingredients tumbling out of the pot

SMALL POTS lie casually by the side of the larger one, completing the autumnal composition

STRONG, BUSHY SEDUM is pushed into wet foam within the large pot

SHINY RED APPLES are attached to the foam with large hairpin hooks

TRADITIONAL CHRISTMAS WREATH

USING A VARIETY of natural festive decorations, this Christmas wreath is simple to make, yet highly effective. The secret is to keep the look simple and avoid crowding on too many decorations. Be selective in your choice of materials and, before starting, plan carefully how to combine and place them. The balsam used here will last for around one month if kept cool.

17in (42cm)

17in (42cm)

DESIGN TIP
The clusters of cones and seed pods create a triangular formation. Likewise, the large red bow is balanced by the bunches of cinnamon wrapped in the same ribbon, forming an opposing triangular shape.

MATERIALS AND EQUIPMENT

Cinnamon sticks are wired in threes, then bound in red ribbon. The other decorations are also wired ready to attach to the wreath (see page 177).

THE FINISHED EFFECT
A rich, traditional, and festive Christmas wreath. Selective use of attractive natural decorations, combined with the rich wine red ribbon, creates a welcoming seasonal door display.

Foliage and decoration

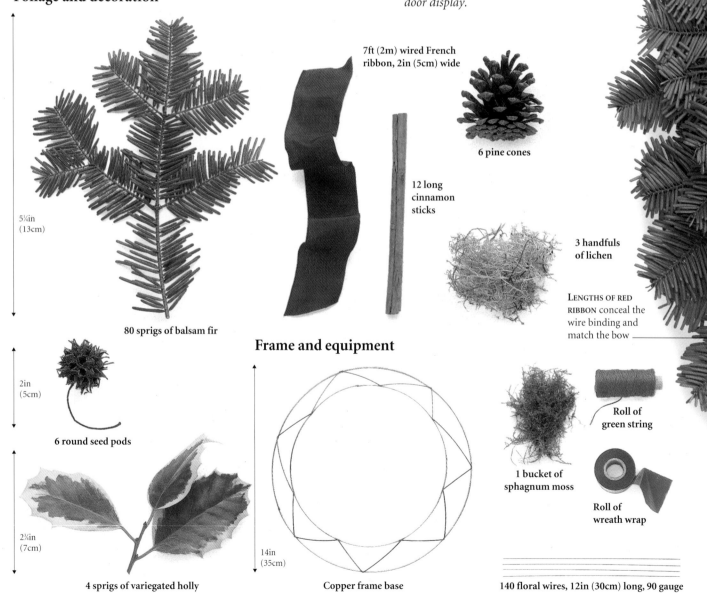

5¼in (13cm)

80 sprigs of balsam fir

7ft (2m) wired French ribbon, 2in (5cm) wide

12 long cinnamon sticks

6 pine cones

3 handfuls of lichen

LENGTHS OF RED RIBBON conceal the wire binding and match the bow

2in (5cm)

6 round seed pods

Frame and equipment

Roll of green string

1 bucket of sphagnum moss

Roll of wreath wrap

2¾in (7cm)

4 sprigs of variegated holly

14in (35cm)

Copper frame base

140 floral wires, 12in (30cm) long, 90 gauge

GROUPS OF DECORATIONS are equally spaced

CONES are individually wired and grouped closely together in threes, leaving no gaps between

CINNAMON STICKS, bound into groups of three with a floral wire, add color and scent

LICHEN acts not only as filler, but adds silver highlights

VARIEGATED HOLLY SPRIGS impart extra color and shine

MAKING THE WREATH

Sphagnum moss is bound to a copper frame with string, and floral wires are used to attach wired balsam and decorations (see page 177). Save the most attractive sprigs for the top of the wreath.

TRIM MOSS off neatly

BIND SPHAGNUM MOSS to the frame with string

FOLD THE WREATH WRAP back and forth on the top of the wreath and attach with hooks

SHORT FLORAL wires cut in half to form hooks

1 Tie the string to the frame. Then press compacted handfuls of sphagnum moss to the frame, binding them on with the string and keeping the moss equally thick all way around. When the frame is covered, tie the string to it with a secure knot.

2 Trim off the moss neatly and turn the frame over. Attach the end of the wreath wrap to the outer edge with floral wires cut in half and bent into hairpin hooks (see page 177). Fold the wrap back and forth diagonally, hooking it to the moss.

PUSH WIRED SPRIGS of balsam into the moss

3 Turn the frame over ag[...] Push the first wired spr[...] of balsam into the mos[...] the outside of the frame, angle[...] the left. Repeat, making sure e[...] sprig overlaps the previous one, [...] form a border about 2¾in (7cm[...] wide around the frame. Then do [...] the same on the inside of the frame

MAKE THE FIRST ring of balsam on the outside of the frame

LAY THE TOP ROW of sprigs between the outer and inner rows

THE WIRE binding the cinnamon sticks is concealed with red ribbon

4 Add the most attractive balsam sprigs to the center of the wreath, to cover the remaining visible moss. Overlap the sprigs in the same direction as the others. Then make a double bow (see page 182) with the wired French ribbon.

5 Attach the bow using a double leg mount (see page 177). Finally, attach two groups of cinnamon sticks bound with red ribbon to create a triangular formation with the bow. Group the other decorations between these points, as shown.

Alternative Combination

The moss-covered frame forms a base that you can decorate with practically anything you wish. Here, for a very different effect, yet just as festive, the base has been covered with sprigs of holly and decorated with gold-painted globe artichokes and a large green and gold bow.

Alternative foliage and decoration

20 bushy sprigs of holly

4 gold-painted globe artichokes

3¼ft (1m) green and gold wired French ribbon, 4in (10cm) wide

GREEN AND GOLD WREATH
The dark green and gold colors complement each other perfectly. Painted globe artichokes stand out starkly from the base of dark, waxy holly leaves, enriched by the sumptuous green and gold ribbon.

HOLLY SPRIGS replace the balsam

FESTIVE FRUIT SWAG

EXTRAVAGANT AND OPULENT, this swag, embellished with a sumptuous selection of foliage and fruit, makes a perfect holiday display. I have used ruffled russet silk to enhance the rich reds and browns of the dates, plums, grapes, and pears to create an effect of imperial grandeur.

MATERIALS AND EQUIPMENT
Foliage and decoration

7¼in (18cm)

ONE STRIP OF SILK is folded to make a wide bow

4 strips of Thai silk, each 10in x 5ft (25cm x 1.5m)

15 sprigs of berried ivy, some sprayed gold

20 generous sprigs of green holly

8 lengths of eucalyptus

2lb (1kg) black and red grapes

5 large plums

4 red pears

8 large fresh dates

10in (25cm)

5 sprigs of trailing ivy

5 sprigs of bog myrtle

BERRIED IVY is highlighted with spray paint for an extra touch

SPRIGS OF FOLIAGE are used around the edge of the garland and as a filler

MAKING THE SWAG

Sandwich sphagnum moss between chicken wire to form a band. Gather two lengths of silk and attach along the band with long floral wires formed into hairpin hooks (see page 177). Then make bows with the remaining silk (see page 182) and attach to each end. Wire the foliage and fruit (see page 177) and attach to the band.

Fold chicken wire around the moss to create the base band

ATTACH FRUIT AND FOLIAGE by working from one end of the band to the other

GROUP FRUIT by type along the length of the swag

PIN RUFFLED SILK to the moss and wire band with hairpin hooks before adding foliage

Equipment

Chicken wire, 14in x 5ft (35cm x 1.5m)

3 buckets of sphagnum moss

100 floral wires, 14in (35cm) long, 90 gauge

THE FINISHED SWAG

The richness of the fabric, fruit, and foliage can be displayed to best effect if the swag is suspended from a prominent mantelpiece. Use hooks to hang up the swag, inserted into the wire and moss behind each bow.

FRAGRANT RED PEARS are attached with wires to the middle of the garland for lighter color contrast

5ft (1.5m)

ARRANGING DRIED FLOWERS

The art of dried flower arranging has changed dramatically in recent times, and the past association with rustic themes has given way to a bolder, more stylized approach. Dried flowers look most effective when massed together, and introducing fabric, raffia, and ribbon often strengthens the design statement. Your choice of container is especially important with dried displays: look for unusual textures and shapes that complement the flowers.

MASSED ROSE DISPLAY
A weathered terra-cotta pot has been filled with a compact mass of dried red roses. The leaves create a band of green color, and a few coils of natural rope add a rustic touch to the formal bunch. The symmetry and bold coloring of this display make it a stunning focal point in any setting.

SMALL-SCALE ARRANGEMENTS

THE DAYS OF PRECIOUS WICKER BASKETS filled with dried sea lavender and tied with pretty country bows are, I am pleased to say, over. Small dried flower arrangements have reached new heights with an emphasis on solid expanses of color, sculptural shapes, and an innovative mix of varieties. For me, an even, compact mass of flower heads, bound with raffia or cord and carved into spheres or bundles, looks far more impressive and impromptu than the shapeless displays that we have seen for so long. Small stylish dried displays make excellent gifts, too, since they can be prepared well in advance and far outlast any fresh arrangement.

As with all types of flower arrangement, the container you work with plays a major part in the final look of the composition. It is even more important when arranging dried flowers; because ingredients are unlikely to spill over and conceal the container, it will be more conspicuous. Plain but bold-colored vases and pots are especially suitable when bunching material like strawflowers into small clumps of single colors. Terra-cotta pots or baskets can be painted to accentuate the sense of density and compactness that suits dried flower displays so well. Glass is surprisingly effective, too, and the naturally bare, spiky stems of dried flowers can be concealed by filling the container with raffia or potpourri.

Evoke movement in small dried arrangements to avoid a feeling of stiffness. Gathered fabric, such as muslin, or knotted raffia form flowing lines when incorporated into a display. You can also use accessories to heighten a theme. A basket wrapped in rope and filled with shells or bleached driftwood has nautical connotations that are appropriate for a bathroom. Christmas displays of gilded blooms and foliage sculpted into miniature forms look more dramatic when adorned with glistening ribbons. And don't forget scent. Flowers such as lavender and roses have a sweet, long-lasting perfume.

Dried flower displays, too, often require florist's foam to provide support and make possible a wide variety of shapes and styles. Always use the dry gray variety: the green foam must be soaked and is suitable only for fresh flowers.

Circular Centerpiece
Page 120

Small Vase Display
Page 126

Seaside Basket
Page 130

Topiary Trees
Page 136

Country Wreath
Page 138

CIRCULAR CENTERPIECE

SELECTIVE USE OF INGREDIENTS creates maximum impact for smaller dried arrangements. Choose flowers of the same color or shape and arrange them evenly throughout the display. Here, bold sunflowers, softened by sheet moss, reflect the color and curved contours of the bowl.

MATERIALS AND EQUIPMENT

The sunflowers and moss are built up on a block of dry foam secured in the bowl with florist's tape.

Flowers and foliage

12in
(30cm)

12 small handfuls of sheet moss

12 sunflowers

10in
(25cm)

12¾in (32cm)

DESIGN TIP
Do not build up the arrangement too far – keep it as high as the bowl is deep. The outline is an even dome shape, and the final display is wider than it is high for a balanced effect.

THE MOSS introduces a natural element into the stylized arrangement

SUNFLOWER HEADS obscure the rim of the bowl

Container and equipment

Block of dry foam taped to round bowl

5¼in
(13cm)

6¾in (17cm)

6 floral wires, 12½in (31cm) long, 90 gauge

THE FINISHED EFFECT
Sunflowers have a dazzling splendor, their glowing yellow harvest colors blending perfectly with a simple golden bowl.

FEATHERY SHEET MOSS acts as a foil to the large, solid, round flowers

A YELLOW CERAMIC BOWL mirrors the color and shape of the sunflowers

MAKING THE CENTERPIECE
Sunflowers are simply pushed into dry foam, row upon row,
while sheet moss is attached with hairpin hooks (see page 177).

ANGLE THE SUNFLOWER
head to jut over the
rim of the bowl

ALTERNATE sunflowers
and handfuls of
sheet moss

*1 Trim the sunflowers at a slant to 4in (10cm),
and push one into the side of the dry foam.
Cut the floral wires in half and bend into
hairpin hooks (see page 177). Use one to hook a
handful of sheet moss next to the sunflower head.*

*2 Push a second sunflower into the foam
next to the moss. Hook another clump of
moss to the foam on the other side of the
first sunflower with a hairpin hook and push in
another sunflower next to that.*

KEEP sunflower
heads level

KEEP THE MOSS and
sunflowers close together

ANGLE HEADS to create
a dome shape

*3 Complete the ring around the rim
of the bowl, alternating sunflowers
and handfuls of sheet moss. Seven
sunflowers and seven handfuls of moss
comprise this first row.*

PUSH IN THE FLOWERS above and between those of the first row

4 *Alternating sunflowers and moss again, start the second row, angling the heads to create a dome shape. Finally, add a single sunflower in the middle of the second row to form the top of the dome.*

Alternative Combination

The mood of the sunflowers can be changed to a softer effect by substituting peonies in subtle shades of pink. A bold turquoise bowl complements the pink flowers and ensures that this display is as strong visually as the first.

Alternative flowers

25 peonies

PEONIES are distributed evenly around the dome

PINK PEONIES
Old-fashioned peonies and a deep-colored bowl create a more formal display that can suit many settings, not only the center of a table.

SHEET MOSS is retained

Scented Centerpiece

The strong sculptural shape of this display is achieved by building up the ingredients in the same way as in the project on pages 120–123. Dried oranges and globe artichoke heads are attached in groups, with bunches of dried red roses pushed in alongside to augment the scent. Handfuls of bun moss fill any gaps and soften the display. Delicate dabs of gold paint add a festive touch to the wintry arrangement, while a trail of gold-sprayed raffia tied to a bunch of roses beside the bowl brings a feeling of movement to the rounded oranges and globe artichokes.

DRIED RED ROSES provide depth of color as well as a sweet scent

FRAGRANT ORANGES have been slit before being dried, echoing the ribbing on the terra-cotta saucer

A BUNCH of roses, bound with raffia, complements the main display

A TRAIL of gold-tinted raffia brings a flowing line to an otherwise static display

DELICATE BRUSHSTROKES of
gold paint make the wintry
display more festive

BUN MOSS fills gaps and
softens the strong outlines
of the arrangement

SMALL VASE DISPLAY

DRIED FLOWER STEMS sometimes look awkward through clear glass, so here I have supported stems of lavender on dry foam, and filled in the tank with potpourri. The resulting arrangement is not only stunning in its simplicity, but also smells heavenly. Use the most fragrant, full-bodied, and deeply colored lavender you can find.

MATERIALS AND EQUIPMENT

The potpourri can easily be replaced when its scent has faded, or you can add scented oil to revive it.

Flowers and decoration

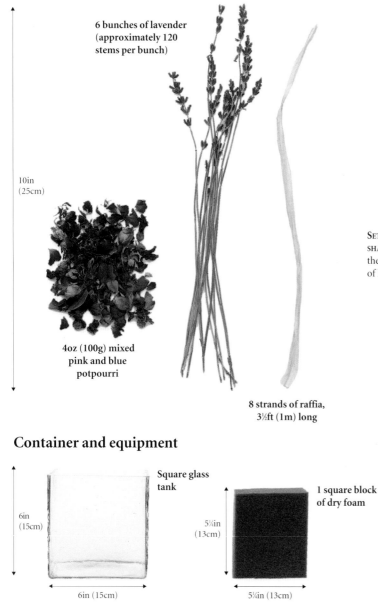

6 bunches of lavender (approximately 120 stems per bunch)

10in (25cm)

4oz (100g) mixed pink and blue potpourri

8 strands of raffia, 3½ft (1m) long

Container and equipment

6in (15cm)

6in (15cm)

Square glass tank

5¼in (13cm)

5¼in (13cm)

1 square block of dry foam

MAKING THE DISPLAY

The foam block almost fills the tank, to reduce the amount of potpourri needed and to create a large surface area for the lavender stems.

FILL IN THE SPACE between the tank and the dry foam with potpourri

1 Place the dry foam in the tank. Fill out the space at the sides with potpourri up to the top of the foam.

SET THE SHAPE with the first row of lavender

2 Push the lavender stems into the foam in a row across the center and add another row to create a cross. Keeping aside about ten stems, fill in the cross to form a compact, domed mass.

ADD MORE POTPOURRI to cover any foam that is showing

3 Wrap the raffia around the tank, and tie it in a single knot. Hold a small bunch of lavender against this knot, and tie it to the tank with the free strands of raffia.

KEEP THE STRANDS OF RAFFIA rough-looking to add a rustic touch

ANGLE THE SMALL BUNCH of lavender away from the main group to balance the arrangement

Container Displays

Vases and containers are especially important when arranging small-scale dried flower displays, since the stems need either to be concealed or made into a feature. The stiffness of dried flowers can pose problems, but it also makes them ideal for topiary trees and compact, massed displays such as these. Decorative bindings can be wound around the stems to break up the starkness further, and moss effectively softens the base of the displays.

DOMED PODS
Mauve-tinted poppy pods have been pushed into dry foam to form a domed mass above a flared galvanized metal container.

SCENTED LAVENDER
Lavender is bound tightly with natural raffia and supported in lichen.

A SUNFLOWER HEAD lies next to the trunk for visual balance

LAVENDER is cut down short for a small, balanced display

A METAL VASE mirrors the mauve poppy pods

128

SUNFLOWER TREE

Sunflower stems, bound to form a tree shape, have been secured in dry foam within a glass tank. Coiled raffia conceals the foam, and sheet moss softens the base of the trunk.

TIMOTHY PALM

Stems of timothy bound into a palmlike shape with raffia sprout from a stained pot. Luxurious bun moss brings out the pale green of the timothy.

STRAWFLOWER BUSH

A painted terra-cotta pot accentuates the dark reddish strawflowers, while light pink raffia binds the stems and connects the two shades of red.

BUN MOSS adds a natural touch to the sumptuous effect

PINK RAFFIA breaks up the line of the stems and introduces a light touch

SEASIDE BASKET

CONTRASTING TEXTURES AND SHAPES in sandy, seaside colors can be juxtaposed to make a spontaneous, eye-catching arrangement that would suit a bathroom or a beach house. Coarse rope, which is used to conceal a plastic container, underpins the nautical theme.

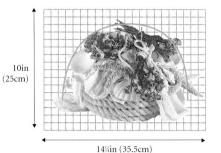

10in (25cm)

14¼in (35.5cm)

DESIGN TIP
The arrangement is wider than it is high, and dome-shaped. Bunches of roses enlarge and fill out the shape.

MATERIALS AND EQUIPMENT

The plastic container is disguised by coiling rope around it, then covered with an unusual combination of shells, starfish, and roses.

Flowers and decoration

8in (20cm)

Thick rope, 5ft (1.5m)

Muslin, 12in x 6½ft (30cm x 2m)

3 starfish

3 polished Venus clams

6 medium-sized scallop shells

8in (20cm)

1 fluted clam

String, 6½ft (2m)

3 bunches of dried roses

MUSLIN is gathered and hooked on-to the dry foam with floral wires shaped into hairpin hooks

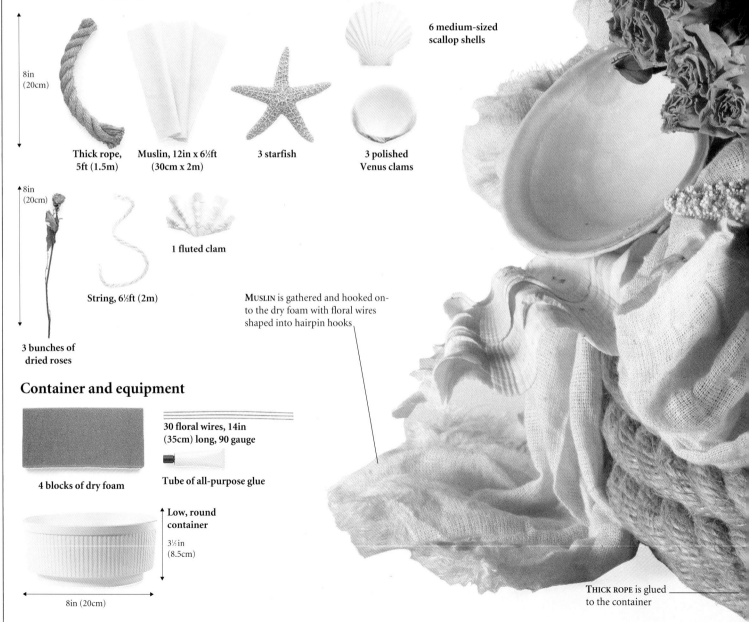

Container and equipment

4 blocks of dry foam

30 floral wires, 14in (35cm) long, 90 gauge

Tube of all-purpose glue

Low, round container

3½in (8.5cm)

8in (20cm)

THICK ROPE is glued to the container

A LENGTH OF ROUGH STRING
disguises the wire binding the
roses, and weaves decoratively
through the arrangement

THE FINISHED EFFECT
*Sandy colors and coarse rope
combine with the peach roses
and varied shells to evoke a
sun-bleached, nautical effect.*

SMOOTH, ROUND VENUS CLAMS
contrast with the rugged
surface of the starfish

SCALLOP SHELLS
complement the
pattern of the heavy
rope around the
container

ALTERNATIVE COMBINATION

The color theme can be changed from peachy coral to gray-green by substituting oregano for the roses and using metallic blue shells. The white scallops are retained to keep the highlights.

3 large abalone shells

5 bunches of dried oregano

10 smaller shells

COIL THE ROPE around the container to conceal the sides

GATHER THE MUSLIN into loose ruffles and hook to the dry foam

1 Starting at the base, dab glue on the container and firmly press the end of the rope against it. Continue gluing and pressing on the rope, coiling it up around the sides of the container to cover it completely. Allow to dry for 20 minutes.

2 Completely fill the container with cut blocks of dry foam, up to 2in (5cm) above the rim. Loosely drape muslin over the top and sides, gathering it in places, and pin it into the foam with floral wires shaped into hairpin hooks (see page 177).

3 Attach the large abalone shells by pushing hairpin hooks through the natural holes in each shell into the dry foam. You may need more than one wire per shell. Attach one shell to the top of the arrangement and two to the sides.

HOOK LARGE ABALONE SHELLS to the top and sides of the dry foam

GROUP THE SCALLOPS in pairs at the sides and top of the arrangement

ANGLE THE SIDE SHELLS to slope downward

ATTACH THE FIRST BUNCH OF HERBS at an angle across the top

USE A SINGLE LENGTH OF STRING to bind the bunches of herbs to one another

4 Glue hairpin hooks to the scallop shells and pin into the foam, or simply push into the foam in pairs between the abalones at the sides and top of the arrangement. Each pair of shells should be angled in the same direction.

5 Divide the oregano into five bunches. Bind each bunch with wires twisted into a double leg mount (see page 177) and push the wires into the foam. Use the length of string to link them, tying it around the bunches.

6 Finally, glue hairpin hooks to the small shells and push the wires into the foam between the larger decorations.

GLUE HAIRPIN HOOKS to small shells, then push them into the foam

Autumnal Gift Basket

Bunches of roses, poppy pods, strawflowers, and peonies have been spiraled and wired to a basket, as in the project on pages 130–133. To complement the dried bunches, a dry foam sphere covered with overlapping silvery eucalyptus leaves fills the back of the basket, while dark red strawflower heads coat a smaller globe next to it. The rich reds, muted grays, and shades of mauve blend with the natural tones of the basket.

MAUVE-TINTED poppy pods help the stark reds to blend with the beige basket

FLORAL WIRES binding the dried bunches are concealed with string

THE LID OF THE BASKET holds bunches of roses and poppy pods

EUCALYPTUS LEAVES arc attached to a dry foam globe with hairpin hooks

LICHEN fills gaps around the flowers and the ball of eucalyptus leaves

A GLOBE OF STRAWFLOWERS completes the composition

TOPIARY TREES

TOPIARY TREES LOOK MOST EFFECTIVE when kept simple: aim for clear outlines and bold shapes for a striking sculptural image. Strong, intensely colored materials create a masculine effect, while paler, delicate flowers in a soft-colored container evoke a pretty, feminine mood.

MATERIALS AND EQUIPMENT

Cement comes as a powder. When water is added it forms a viscous mixture that sets quickly around the branches.

Flowers and decoration

12in (30cm)

3 sections of branches

100 stems of achillea

3 handfuls of sheet moss

Container and equipment

Decorative plant pot

6¾in (17cm)

6¾in (17cm)

10 handfuls of sphagnum moss

Black plastic, 10 x 10in (25 x 25cm)

2lb (1kg) cement mix

Reel of florist's wire

50 floral wires, 10½in (26cm) long, 71 gauge

MAKING THE ARRANGEMENT

THREE BRANCH SECTIONS are secured in cement to form the trunk

SPHAGNUM MOSS is secured with florist's wire

THE POT is lined with black plastic to protect it from the cement

START ADDING ACHILLEA from the top of the moss globe

ACHILLEA HEAD in a double leg mount

1 *Line the pot with black plastic. Fill it with mixed cement up to ¾in (2cm) below the rim. Push in the sections of branches and allow to set. Trim off the plastic just above the cement.*

2 *Wind the florist's wire around the exposed ends of the branches to secure them. Press handfuls of sphagnum moss to the top of the trunk, winding the wire around them to form a moss globe.*

3 *Trim the achillea to 2in (5cm) and wire in a double leg mount (see page 177) with floral wires cut in half. Push them into the moss to cover it completely. Add sheet moss around the base of the trunk.*

THE FINISHED TREE
The smooth, architectural look of the larger tree (center below) is enhanced by grouping it with smaller trees made in the same way.

KEEP THE GLOBE smooth by pressing in any protruding flower heads gently with your palm

SHEET MOSS conceals the cement and adds a natural touch

COUNTRY WREATH

A DRIED WREATH MAKES A SPLENDID DISPLAY at any time of the year, whether used indoors or hung outdoors during dry weather. Here, the colors in a summery printed fabric are echoed with rich red roses, velvety sheet moss, and supple amaranthus. The muted colors of the lighter roses help the dark reds to fuse with the pale poppy pods, softening the overall effect.

MATERIALS AND EQUIPMENT

Fabric adds fullness and movement to the wreath, and the roses are chosen to match.

Flowers and decoration

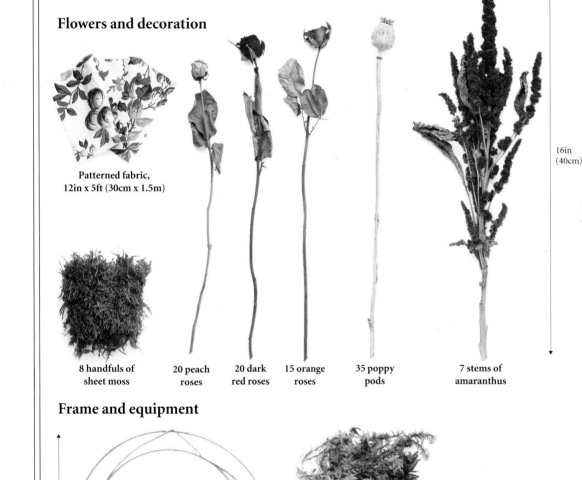

LARGER POPPY PODS are grouped toward the top of the wreath

16in (40cm)

Patterned fabric, 12in x 5ft (30cm x 1.5m)

8 handfuls of sheet moss

20 peach roses

20 dark red roses

15 orange roses

35 poppy pods

7 stems of amaranthus

Frame and equipment

8½in (21cm)

Copper frame base

8 handfuls of sphagnum moss

Roll of green string

15 floral wires, 10½in (26cm) long, 90 gauge

120 floral wires, 12½in (31cm) long, 71 gauge

THE FINISHED EFFECT
*A rich, opulent wreath, yet still light
and summery and full of movement.
The patterned fabric adds a country
feel to an otherwise quite
formal arrangement.*

PEACH-COLORED ROSES
link the faded poppy pods
with the dark red roses
and amaranthus

DARK GREEN SHEET MOSS
echoes the greens in the fabric

PATTERNED COUNTRY FABRIC
weaves between the groups
of flowers and moss

MAKING THE WREATH

Moss is bound to a frame with string instead of using a dry foam ring. This creates a sturdier, longer-lasting base that puts important flower-arranging skills into practice.

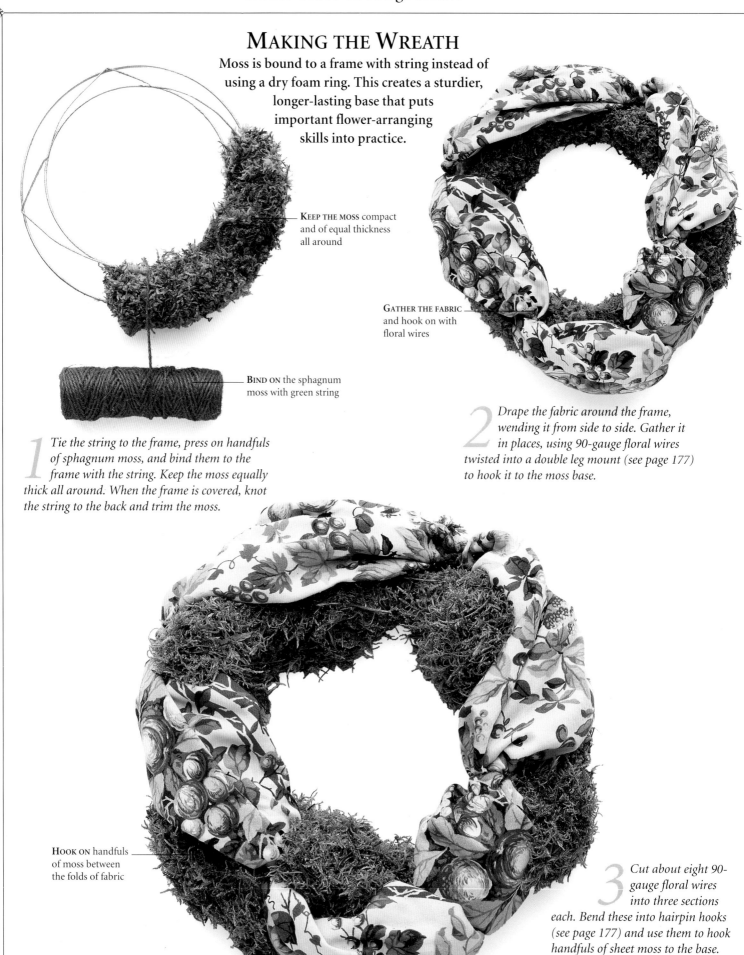

KEEP THE MOSS compact and of equal thickness all around

GATHER THE FABRIC and hook on with floral wires

BIND ON the sphagnum moss with green string

1 Tie the string to the frame, press on handfuls of sphagnum moss, and bind them to the frame with the string. Keep the moss equally thick all around. When the frame is covered, knot the string to the back and trim the moss.

2 Drape the fabric around the frame, wending it from side to side. Gather it in places, using 90-gauge floral wires twisted into a double leg mount (see page 177) to hook it to the moss base.

HOOK ON handfuls of moss between the folds of fabric

3 Cut about eight 90-gauge floral wires into three sections each. Bend these into hairpin hooks (see page 177) and use them to hook handfuls of sheet moss to the base.

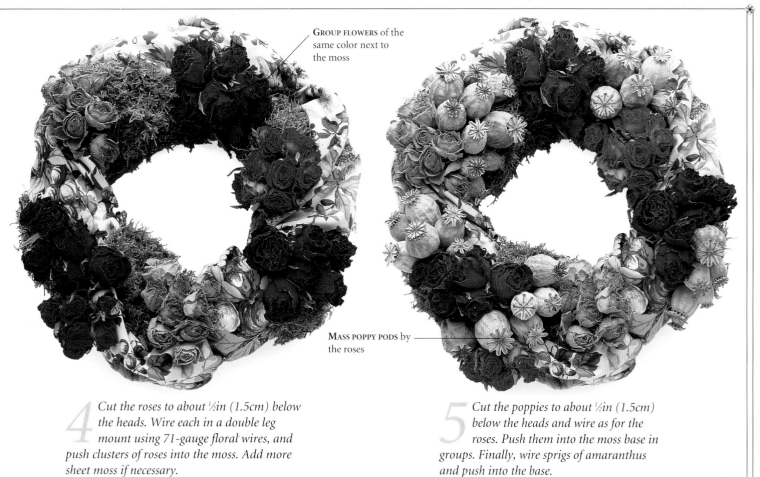

GROUP FLOWERS of the same color next to the moss

MASS POPPY PODS by the roses

4 Cut the roses to about ½in (1.5cm) below the heads. Wire each in a double leg mount using 71-gauge floral wires, and push clusters of roses into the moss. Add more sheet moss if necessary.

5 Cut the poppies to about ½in (1.5cm) below the heads and wire as for the roses. Push them into the moss base in groups. Finally, wire sprigs of amaranthus and push into the base.

Alternative Combination

By removing the roses, amaranthus, and sheet moss, and substituting achillea, wheat, and lichen, the emphasis can be changed from a rich, summery red to warm, ocher harvest colors.

Alternative flowers and foliage

20 stems of achillea

100 stems of wheat

5 handfuls of lichen

ACHILLEA changes the dominant color from red to yellow

THE FABRIC IS RETAINED, but still links in with the new colors

HARVEST WREATH
The floral fabric and poppy pods have been retained, but mustard-colored achillea and sandy heads of wheat replace the roses and amaranthus to create a more casual country feel.

ROSE BASKET DISPLAY
Bright roses, staggered down from the back to the front in blocks of color, fill a large rustic basket. An additional bunch of roses is bound to one of the handles with decorative rope.

LARGE-SCALE ARRANGEMENTS

LARGE ARRANGEMENTS OF DRIED FLOWERS are as versatile as they are long-lasting. Hanging bunches, country displays, formal swags, and open basket arrangements not only lift an occasion or seasonal celebration but can remain *in situ* as a permanent year-round decoration. The larger scale allows room to experiment with textural variety, contrasting shapes, and daring color combinations. As with small-scale dried flower arrangements, I prefer to group flower varieties by type, but rather than producing compact clumps of color, I aim for more open, freer shapes.

Bunches of dried and drying flowers suspended from a ceiling, wall, or cupboard door make wonderful, glowing displays that are extremely simple to assemble. Select dried materials with strong color variations, perhaps even clashes of color, and think about interesting textural combinations. The smooth, yet brittle, surface of poppy pods, for example, is an excellent foil for softer or more feathery flowers, such as lamb's-ears or timothy. As with all arrangements, bear in mind the final setting of hanging bunches during their preparation: if suspended from the ceiling they will be viewed from below.

Flatter and wider bouquets of dried flowers can be laid in painted wooden fruit baskets and look particularly apt placed on a kitchen floor. Sculptural vegetables, such as rounded artichoke heads and heavy corncobs, can be used to accentuate the harvest or rustic theme.

You can also celebrate the changing seasons with large dried arrangements. A wheat sheaf has a natural simplicity perfect for Thanksgiving or harvest celebrations, while garlands containing white birch, lichen, and achillea make imaginative winter or Christmas displays that can be enjoyed year after year.

More complicated dried arrangements may require some technical equipment: chicken wire wrapped around dried foam is an essential aid, as are accessories such as decorative string, furnishing fabric, and colored braid to disguise wires and bind flowers together.

Wheat Sheaf Decoration
Page 144

Hanging Bunches
Page 146

Winter Garland
Page 148

Summer Wooden Basket
Page 152

WHEAT SHEAF DECORATION

THE WHEAT SHEAF IS A TIMELESS SYMBOL and a classic form of decoration. Whether freestanding or hung on the wall, a large wheat sheaf makes a year-round decoration that will fit into any setting, whether formal, traditional, rustic, or modern. It would be particularly appropriate for harvest time or Thanksgiving Day.

MATERIALS AND EQUIPMENT
Choose binding fabric for the wheat sheaf to complement its surroundings.

Wheat and fabric

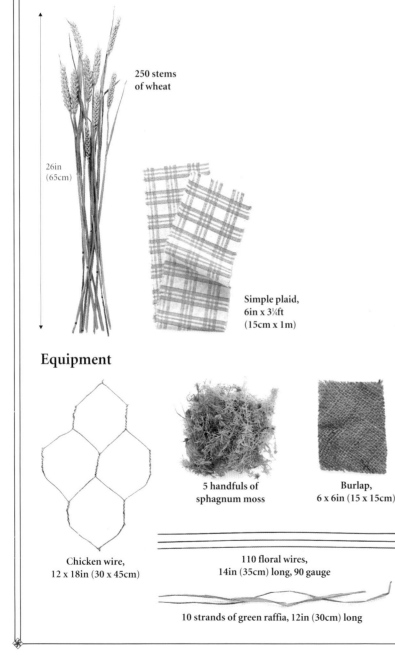

26in
(65cm)

250 stems
of wheat

Simple plaid,
6in x 3¼ft
(15cm x 1m)

Equipment

Chicken wire,
12 x 18in (30 x 45cm)

5 handfuls of
sphagnum moss

Burlap,
6 x 6in (15 x 15cm)

110 floral wires,
14in (35cm) long, 90 gauge

10 strands of green raffia, 12in (30cm) long

SIMPLE PLAID FABRIC completes the harvest feel and brings out the subtle coloring of the wheat

THE FINISHED EFFECT
The studied simplicity and minimum use of decoration achieve an effect of natural sophistication that will blend with informal and formal environments alike.

MAKING THE ARRANGEMENT

As you work, keep checking the arrangement from the front and sides to make sure you are building up the rows evenly all around.

USE THE STRANDS OF RAFFIA to hang up the finished wheat sheaf

Back view

1 Wrap the sphagnum moss in chicken wire to form a compact square. Secure with floral wires bent into hairpin hooks (see page 177). Pin burlap to the back in the same way. Twist raffia around hairpins and hook to the top corners.

MAKE THE SECOND ROW slightly shorter than the first

2 Cut the wheat stems in half, and group the heads into bunches of five. Trim to the length you require, double leg mount them (see page 177), and push into the moss in four arched rows, each row shorter than the last.

3 Cut the wheat stalks to one length, double leg mount them in groups of five, and push into the bottom of the base in four rows. Make a bow (see page 182), fray the ends, and attach with wires between the heads of wheat and the stalks.

TRIM THE STALKS to produce a curved fan shape

FIVE STALKS bound in a double leg mount

HANGING BUNCHES

FOR STUNNING WALL DECORATIONS, nothing could be simpler to make than hanging bunches of dried flowers. Group flowers by type, aiming for interesting color coordinations, and contrasts of shape and texture. Bind the bunches with complementary string, ribbon, or rope.

NATURAL, COARSE STRING adds a rustic touch

COOL SHADES
Mauve poppy pods and hydrangeas link the silvery lamb's-ears and dark purple lavender. The smoothness of the poppies and velvety lamb's-ears are an interesting textural contrast.

THE GRAY-GREEN RIBBON highlights the shades in the flowers

VIBRANT TONES
Tomato red roses, pink peonies, and coral-toned atriplex form a stylish, harmonious bouquet. The lighter peonies break up the darker reds, and the long stems of atriplex form an attractive and practical base for the other rounded flowers.

DARK LAVENDER gives the bunch depth as well as scent

SMOOTH POPPY PODS add solidity to the bunch

HARVEST BOUQUET
Heavy corncobs, sunflower heads, and globe artichokes are set off by delicate seedheads and feathery timothy. Note how the large rounded heads contrast with the long thinner plants. This sort of bouquet would look equally effective if laid in a low country basket.

RICH GOLDEN BRAID accentuates the sunflowers and corncobs

ROUNDED SUNFLOWER HEADS and globe artichokes sit in the center of the bunch

FEATHERY FRONDS OF TIMOTHY offset the dried, parchmentlike husks around the corncobs

WINTER GARLAND

TO ACHIEVE A NATURAL OUTDOORSY LOOK, I have combined delicate lichen and achillea in a winter garland for festive occasions. Try coordinating the fabric with your interior furnishings, using any leftover material. The back of the band can also be lined with fabric, if desired. The garland hangs well from a mantelpiece or from the edge of a table, if suspended from hooks.

MATERIALS AND EQUIPMENT

Lengths of white birch have been sawed off a main branch for this garland, but you can buy ready-cut lengths of wood.

Equipment

Chicken wire,
16in x 6½ft (40cm x 2m)

**4 blocks of
dry foam**

**5 handfuls of
sphagnum moss**

100 floral wires, 14in (35cm) long, 90 gauge

THE FINISHED EFFECT
Cool, gray-green colors complement the sandy rope and white birch to create an attractive alternative to the usual rich, heavy Christmas colors.

CREAM FABRIC has been gathered and hooked onto the dry foam

FLOWERS AND LICHEN,
attached in groups, alternate
from side to side

Flowers, foliage, and decoration

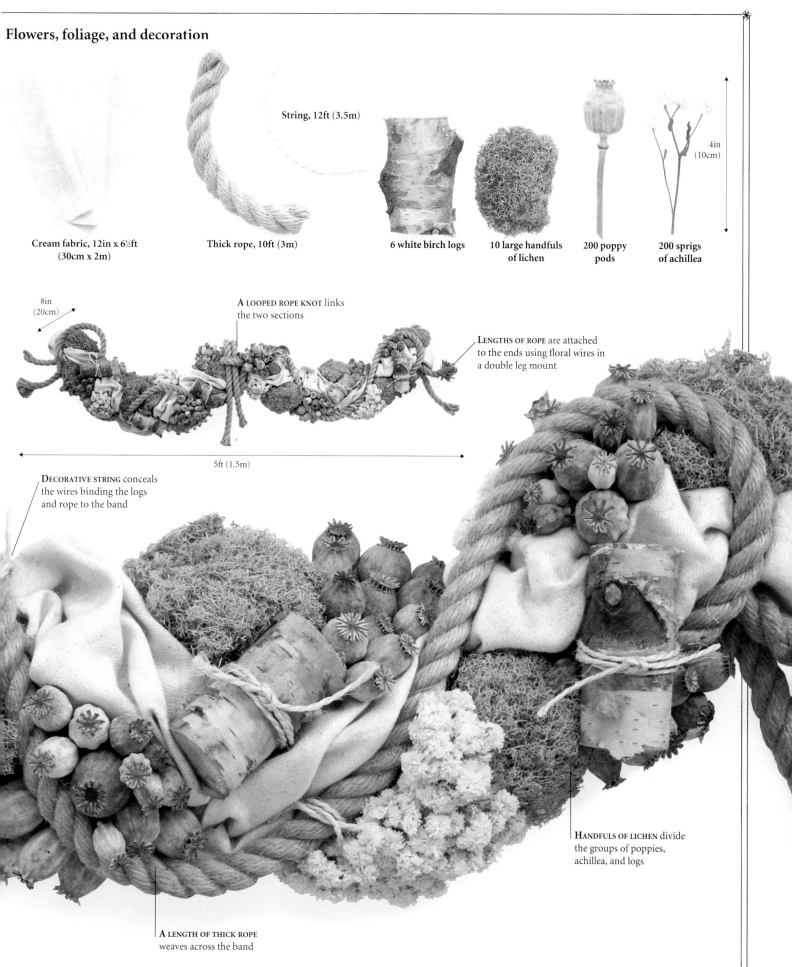

Cream fabric, 12in x 6½ft
(30cm x 2m)

Thick rope, 10ft (3m)

String, 12ft (3.5m)

6 white birch logs

10 large handfuls
of lichen

200 poppy
pods

200 sprigs
of achillea

4in
(10cm)

8in
(20cm)

A LOOPED ROPE KNOT links
the two sections

LENGTHS OF ROPE are attached
to the ends using floral wires in
a double leg mount

5ft (1.5m)

DECORATIVE STRING conceals
the wires binding the logs
and rope to the band

HANDFULS OF LICHEN divide
the groups of poppies,
achillea, and logs

A LENGTH OF THICK ROPE
weaves across the band

MAKING THE GARLAND

The garland is made of two sections that are linked with a
looped rope knot. This avoids a bulky centerpoint, a problem
when one long band is bent into a garland shape.

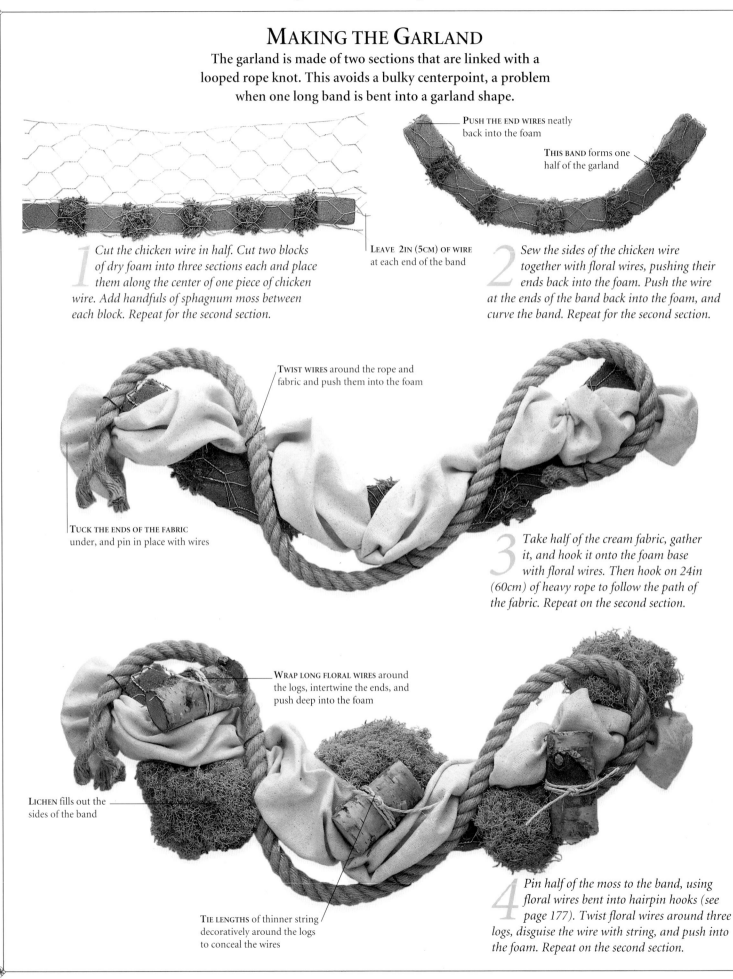

PUSH THE END WIRES neatly
back into the foam

THIS BAND forms one
half of the garland

*1 Cut the chicken wire in half. Cut two blocks
of dry foam into three sections each and place
them along the center of one piece of chicken
wire. Add handfuls of sphagnum moss between
each block. Repeat for the second section.*

LEAVE 2IN (5CM) OF WIRE
at each end of the band

*2 Sew the sides of the chicken wire
together with floral wires, pushing their
ends back into the foam. Push the wire
at the ends of the band back into the foam, and
curve the band. Repeat for the second section.*

TWIST WIRES around the rope and
fabric and push them into the foam

TUCK THE ENDS OF THE FABRIC
under, and pin in place with wires

*3 Take half of the cream fabric, gather
it, and hook it onto the foam base
with floral wires. Then hook on 24in
(60cm) of heavy rope to follow the path of
the fabric. Repeat on the second section.*

WRAP LONG FLORAL WIRES around
the logs, intertwine the ends, and
push deep into the foam

LICHEN fills out the
sides of the band

TIE LENGTHS of thinner string
decoratively around the logs
to conceal the wires

*4 Pin half of the moss to the band, using
floral wires bent into hairpin hooks (see
page 177). Twist floral wires around three
logs, disguise the wire with string, and push into
the foam. Repeat on the second section.*

FLOWERS AND LOGS are clustered within each curve of the rope

GROUP THE POPPY PODS generously around the logs

PUSH ACHILLEA BUNCHES into the foam in groups

5 Trim the poppy pods about 4in (10cm) below the head. Group both small and larger pods together and push half of them into the dry foam in clusters near the logs. Let them nestle into the logs. Repeat on the second section.

6 Wire half of the achillea (see page 177) and push into the foam. Repeat on the second section. Finally, attach two rope tassels to the outer end of each section. Form the remaining rope into a knot, to join the sections.

USE STUB WIRES to attach the tassels and knot to the two sections

Alternative Combination

To make a more traditional festive garland, substitute rich, glowing red fabric and darker, more seasonal decorations. Add brushstrokes of gold paint for a really sumptuous display.

CHRISTMAS GARLAND
Deep red fabric and rich green moss create a classic Christmas combination, enhanced by pine cones, chilies and dabs of gold paint.

Alternative decorations

Red silk, 12in x 6½ft (30cm x 2m)

10 large pieces of sheet moss

4 lengths of stringed chilies (approximately 15 chilies per section)

40 dyed red magnolia leaves

20 pine cones

LIGHT BRUSHSTROKES of gold paint liven up the dark red magnolia leaves, brown pine cones, and chilies

RICH GREEN SHEET MOSS replaces the lighter lichen

DARK RED FABRIC is gathered and swirled, echoing the cone spirals

RED CHILIES are strung together with string through the stems

MAGNOLIA LEAVES are curled under and hooked in place with wires

SUMMER WOODEN BASKET

TO CREATE THE IMPRESSION OF A BOUQUET laid casually in a wooden basket, peonies have been cut in half and pushed into a block of dry foam. A voluminous bow (see page 182) conceals the gap between the flower heads and the lower half of the stems. This subtle display would suit a country kitchen or a feminine-looking bedroom.

PEONIES in delicate pinks and creams create an elegant, feminine image

THE SUBTLE TEAL COLOR of the basket is the perfect backdrop for the opulent flowers

A **LARGE BOW** adds height and imparts a luxurious feel to the simple arrangement

MAKING THE BASKET DISPLAY

Dry foam is secured to the basket with florist's tape, and peony stems are cut in half. The blooms are grouped at one corner, pushed into one end of the foam. The lower halves of the stems are pushed into the corner diagonally opposite. The gap between is concealed with a large bow attached to the foam with floral wires formed into double leg mounts (see page 177).

THE ENDS OF THE BOW drape over the sides of the basket with unaffected elegance

DRIED FLOWERS FOR SPECIAL OCCASIONS

The enduring quality of dried flowers is particularly valuable for those special celebrations that need a great deal of advance planning. Dried flowers can be prepared ahead for Christmas, Easter, Thanksgiving, and weddings. Because these arrangements will keep their color and form for a long time, you will have a beautiful memento of the occasion, particularly if you are imaginative with your use of accessories.

VICTORIAN POSY

WIRED SPRIGS OF ATRIPLEX from a generous band around the achillea

THIS CHARMING AND LONG-LASTING traditional Victorian posy makes a perfect Mother's Day gift, Valentine posy, or a bridesmaid's bouquet. I have chosen the flowers for their different textures and colors to create five distinct rings. Each ring is angled out from the center to keep the posy flat underneath and slightly domed above.

MATERIALS AND EQUIPMENT

You need only one rose bloom, but plenty of rose leaves, so incorporate leftover flower heads into another arrangement.

Flowers and foliage

14in (35cm)

| 1 red rose head plus 35 rose leaves (about 8 rose stems) | 36 stems of lavender | 20 sprigs of achillea | 4 stems of atriplex |

Equipment

50 floral wires, 7in (17.5cm) long, 30 gauge

10 floral wires, 14in (35cm) long, 56 gauge

Roll of fine florist's tape

30in (75cm) wired French ribbon, 1½in (3.5cm) wide

DELICATE SHADES OF COLOR in the atriplex blend with the green rose leaves, the creamy achillea, and the central red rose

FINE-TOOTHED LEAVES create an attractive border for the bunch of flowers

THE RING OF ACHILLEA forms a slightly wider band and breaks up the darker rings of color

Side view

WIRED RIBBON is bound around the stem, and the ends of the knot cut into a V-shape

BIND WIRED BUNCHES of lavender around the central rose

USE WIRED ROSE LEAVES to support and frame the whole posy, overlapping them slightly to prevent gaps

THE FINISHED EFFECT
Contrasting colors, shapes, and textures keep the bands distinct, while the lavender adds a familiar, delicate scent.

MAKING THE POSY
Wire and bind the rose head and leaves individually, and wire the other flowers into bunches (see pages 177–178).

1 *Cut the lavender stems just beneath the flower heads, and wire into bunches of three stems each. Place them around the central wired rose, keeping the heads level with the rose, and bind them together with the tape at a point 3in (7.5cm) below the flower heads.*

GROUP COMPACT BUNCHES of achillea around the lavender, a little lower down

2 *Cut the achillea stems 1¼in (3cm) beneath the flower heads and wire into bunches. Place around the lavender and rose bunch, so that they lie approximately ½in (1cm) lower than the lavender heads. Bind on with the tape at the same point as in step 1.*

3 *Bind wired bunches of atriplex around the achillea, then a ring of wired rose leaves. Bind flowers and foliage at the same point on the stem – this forces them out, keeping the underside of the posy flat. Finally, bind the stem with ribbon (see page 183).*

Gift Posy

Today's approach to dried flower arranging has come a long way from its traditional roots, and this sophisticated gift posy is a classic example of the new direction the art has taken. The bright, fresh look of the stylized posy, combined with an artfully decorated hatbox, makes a stunning gift for a special occasion and a precious keepsake.

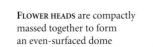

FLOWER HEADS are compactly massed together to form an even-surfaced dome

LEVELED-OFF STEMS make the posy freestanding

STEMS are spirally bound and secured with braided rope

ROSES, CRASPEDIA, AND ACHILLEA in rich golden yellow are combined in random groups

PLAIN TISSUE PAPER has been sprayed gold to add to the luxurious effect

PRESENTATION BOX

The posy fits neatly into an understated brown paper-covered hatbox. Rope similar to that which adorns the posy binds a small decorative bunch of the same flowers to the lid.

WEDDING HEADDRESS

DRIED FLOWERS FOR SPECIAL OCCASIONS can be prepared well in advance, and there is no better time to ease the stress of final preparations than before a wedding. This delicate tiara-shaped headdress celebrates the onset of the rich reds and browns of autumn, making it ideal for a wedding later in the year.

MATERIALS AND EQUIPMENT

Remove stems and excess foliage from the flowers before wiring them (see page 178). Use the two long floral wires to form the main ring.

Flowers

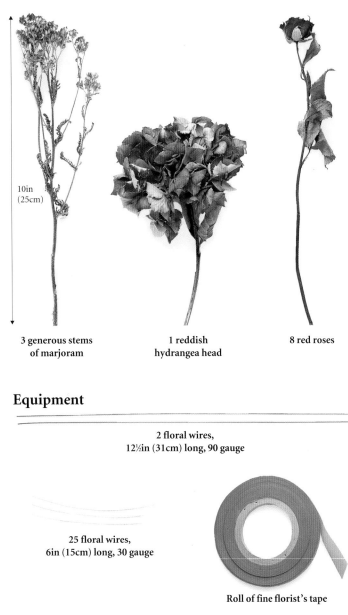

10in
(25cm)

3 generous stems of marjoram

1 reddish hydrangea head

8 red roses

Equipment

**2 floral wires,
12½in (31cm) long, 90 gauge**

**25 floral wires,
6in (15cm) long, 30 gauge**

Roll of fine florist's tape

MAKING THE HEADDRESS

Divide the hydrangea into six sprigs and the marjoram into seven sprigs, then wire and bind each sprig and each rose head individually (see pages 178–180).

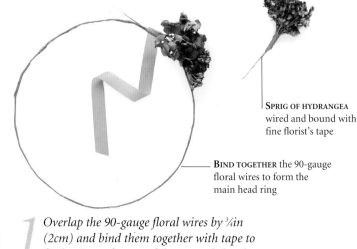

SPRIG OF HYDRANGEA wired and bound with fine florist's tape

BIND TOGETHER the 90-gauge floral wires to form the main head ring

1 Overlap the 90-gauge floral wires by ¾in (2cm) and bind them together with tape to fit the circumference of the wearer's head. Bind on a small wired sprig of marjoram followed by a sprig of hydrangea.

2 Bind on two wired roses, another sprig of marjoram, another hydrangea, and finally a rose. Keep the flowers facing in the same direction, angling the final sprigs farther out, away from the ring.

Wedding Headaddress

3 Starting on the opposite side and facing the other direction, bind on the same flowers in the same order as in steps 1 and 2. This second sequence mirrors the first, and a gap remains between the two.

ATTACH FLOWERS in the same order as on the right side, facing the opposite way

4 To fill the gap between the two sequences, create a tiara effect. Starting on the inner side of each sequence, attach three sprigs of marjoram, two sprigs of hydrangea, and two rose heads, binding them on to stand higher than the other flowers.

ANGLE FLOWERS upward to form the crest of the tiara

THE FINISHED EFFECT

The compactly arranged flowers in the rich headdress form a crest in the middle to create a tiara effect. The unadorned part of the ring is worn beneath the hair at the back of the head, keeping the flowers on top of the head. A veil can be attached to the ring, too.

PETAL BASKET

AS AN ALTERNATIVE to a bowl or wicker basket, this wire container decorated with dried flowers provides an attractive holder for various fillers, from traditional potpourri to fragrant soap, sea shells, or bottles of perfume. The delicate textures and light colors of the larkspur and raffia complement the fine wire and provide an attractive frame around the basket.

STRANDS OF RAFFIA weave along the rim, hooked into moss with floral wires

BUNCHES OF LARKSPUR are bound with wires, knotted with green raffia, then hooked into moss

COLORFUL POTPOURRI shows through the fine mesh

Viewed from above

LAVENDER-BLUE LARKSPUR is attached to point casually in different directions

SHEET MOSS is bound to the rim of the basket with florist's wires

DECORATING THE BASKET

Handfuls of sphagnum moss are bound to the rim of the basket with floral wires. Green raffia weaves around the rim, hooked into the moss at regular intervals. Bunches of larkspur are wired, knotted with raffia, and pushed into the moss.

PINK, RED, AND YELLOW PETALS harmonize beautifully with the lilac larkspur and lime green raffia

ALTERNATIVE FILLERS

Apart from potpourri, the basket can be used to hold a variety of attractive fillers, for display or as gifts.

SCENTED SOAP

Make plain soap look special by wrapping it in deep blue tissue paper and binding it with matching raffia.

EASTER EGGS

Perfect for Easter, the basket makes a delightful "nest" for painted hard-boiled eggs.

SEA SHELLS

For a bathroom decoration, fill the basket with a selection of sea shells.

HARVEST FESTIVAL DISPLAY

THE WARM COLORS AND VARIED TEXTURES of a late summer landscape are immediately brought to mind in this rich harvest display. A cornflower blue wooden crate is laden with bread loaves of various shapes and sizes, juxtaposed with a bundle of wheat angled over one corner. Muted green, mauve, and blue mop-headed hydrangeas echo the rounded shapes of the bread. Tendrils of dried hops arch over the back of the display and weave around the front, and burnished orange Chinese lanterns and golden corncobs evoke the glow of late summer sunshine.

MAKING THE DISPLAY
The wooden crate is filled with blocks of dry foam. Loaves of bread are secured with long hairpin hooks to the side of the foam, and a bushel of wheat is attached behind. The other ingredients build up from this base.

GLOWING CORNCOBS
are grouped on one
side for impact

HOPS arch over the back
of the display and weave
across the front

164

BOLD ORANGE Chinese lanterns uplift the more muted colors

A BUNDLE OF WHEAT echoes the bunches of pale green hops

CHRISTMAS DECORATIONS

CHRISTMAS IS THE TIME TO INDULGE in a spell of creative, festive invention. I like to create bold, opulent arrangements and decorations using richly colored dried flowers and foliage and sumptuous fruit, adorned with flourishes of shimmering gold paint. Ornate ribbons and gold-tinted rope set off the rich colors, while aromatic cloves, candles, and oranges enhance the festive feeling.

CAUTION
If you light the candles, do not leave the arrangement unattended, since dried flowers and decorations are highly flammable.

PAINTED CHRISTMAS BASKET
A simple wooden basket has been painted wine red, packed with dry foam, and filled to bursting with gold-speckled pine cones, chilies, and a pot overflowing with roses, all clustered around three candles.

GOLD-PAINTED STRING decoratively binds the candles and weaves through the arrangement

CONES, LEAVES, and threaded chili garlands are wired and pushed into dry foam

SHEET MOSS enhances the bountiful, natural effect

SIX BANDS OF GOLD braid divide the cloves

Braided Elizabethan pomander

SHINY GOLD RIBBON gleams through the cloves

CLOVE POMANDERS

Traditional Christmas favorites, deliciously scented pomanders can be hung anywhere. Use bright ribbon and shiny braid that will contrast with the dark cloves. Try using kumquats, too, to make tree decorations.

SECTIONS OF ORANGE are left uncovered for bright, radiant decoration

Tartan pomander

Traditional pomander

SMOOTH WAXY MAGNOLIA leaves are pushed into dry foam

DECORATIVE POTS

Dark green dyed magnolia leaves fill one pot and adorn the outside of another, enlivened by sparkling wired ribbon tied into bows.

A HINT OF GOLD is added to the leaves, chilies, and cones

A SCENTED WHITE candle sits on a block of dry foam

GOLD WIRED RIBBON breaks up the rich, dark colors

167

FESTIVE TOPIARY TREES

TOPIARY TREES MAKE DELIGHTFUL, WHIMSICAL holiday decorations that can be adorned in highly individualistic styles. Whether spirited and glitzy, or subtle and understated, these magical trees look especially enchanting when grouped together, the chunky, rounded trees contrasting with the pointed, conical shapes.

A CLUSTER OF CLOVES adorns the peak of the cone

BAY LEAF AND CLOVE TREE
Dried artichoke stems are pushed into dry foam and a piece of conical dry foam is pressed on top. Fresh bay leaves are pinned to overlap each other with short hairpin hooks (see page 177), and rings of sparkling cloves create a fairy-tale-like effect.

GOLDEN GLOBE ARTICHOKE
A globe artichoke, colored with gold paint, is pushed by its stalk into dry foam in a gold-tinted terra-cotta pot. Tangerine-colored wired ribbon is wrapped around the top of the pot.

CLOVES are lighly touched with gold paint

AN ARTICHOKE HEAD is brushed with gold paint

SHEET MOSS conceals the dry foam

THE TERRA-COTTA POT is painted dark green and decorated with gold paint

TOUCHES OF GOLD paint enliven a simple terra-cotta pot

MOSS AND STRING SPHERE

A section of branch has been secured in a pot with cement mix and a sphere of dry foam pushed on top. Sheet moss covers the foam, attached with hairpin hooks (see page 177), and the globe is bound with gold-tinted string.

WIRING DECORATIONS

To wire chestnuts, push a strong floral wire into each one and bend it back. Wire larch cones in a double leg mount (see page 177).

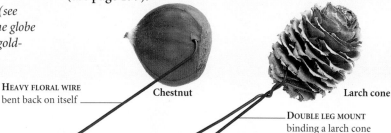

HEAVY FLORAL WIRE bent back on itself

Chestnut

Larch cone

DOUBLE LEG MOUNT binding a larch cone

A THICK SECTION OF branch is secured in the pot with cement

STRING is wound around the pot to match that on the tree

INDIVIDUALLY WIRED chestnuts and cones are pushed into dry foam

CHESTNUTS AND CONES

Chestnuts and larch cones sprout from dry foam to form a compact, rounded topiary tree. A branch of white birch acts as the trunk, pressed into dry foam that is concealed with moss.

AN OLD WEATHERED POT needs no decoration

MATERIALS
& SKILLS

*An understanding of flower arranging
techniques underpins creative flower design
at every level. Applying skills correctly will
enhance your sense of satisfaction with the
finished display. Whether wiring a bloom
or spiraling stems, try not to take any
shortcuts. Good technique will produce
stronger, longer-lasting arrangements,
and your efforts will be rewarded
by the final results.*

ESSENTIAL EQUIPMENT

FOR CREATIVE FLOWER ARRANGING, some basic equipment is essential, both to establish a strong-structured arrangement and to make a wide variety of inventive designs possible. You will not need a vast amount of equipment: included here are all the materials necessary to complete the projects in this book.

FLORAL WIRES

Many lengths and gauges of wire are used in flower arranging. These are the sizes I find most useful:

Fine floral wire, 30 gauge

56 gauge

71 gauge

90 gauge

CHICKEN WIRE
Flexible and strong, chicken wire is useful for binding around foam when making garland bases and for providing extra support in loosely arranged fresh displays.

FLORIST'S WIRE
Florist's wire is fine but strong, making it ideal for wiring longer flowers if floral wires are not long enough and for preventing bulk when binding materials together.

FLORAL WIRES
Fine floral wires are used to reduce bulk and give extra support to delicate flowers. Heavier-gauge wires, such as 71 or 90, are valuable for attaching sturdy materials securely to a base, while medium-gauge wires, such as 56, can be used to secure less sturdy ingredients.

FLORIST'S FOAM
Green florist's foam, or "oasis," should be used only for fresh flower arrangements. Float the foam in water with added flower food to ensure that water soaks right into the center of the block. It is available in a variety of shapes.

Florist's foam

Dry foam

DRY FOAM
Gray dry foam is practical for dried flower displays, and should always be used dry. Available in blocks, rings, cones, and spheres, it can easily be cut to shape.

Wreath frame

WREATH FRAME
When making dried flower wreaths, I prefer to use a copper frame and bind moss to it to form a strong base for attaching flowers and decorations.

FOAM RING
Less sturdy than bound moss on a copper wreath frame, a foam ring can be used wet to provide an ample supply of water for fresh flower displays, and dry for dried flower wreaths and centerpieces.

SAUCER
Wet florist's foam can be secured to a saucer with florist's tape as a base for fresh flower arrangements. The saucer can be placed inside another container.

Foam ring

FLORIST'S TAPE
This strong, waterproof tape sticks to nonporous and shiny surfaces, and is valuable when securing florist's foam and dry foam to a container.

FINE FLORIST'S TAPE
A thin, delicate, rubber-based tape, fine florist's tape seals under pressure and heat. It is ideal for binding and concealing the wired stems of fresh or dried material.

CLEAR ADHESIVE TAPE
An all-purpose clear adhesive tape is useful for making support grids over the mouths of bowls and vases. Flowers are inserted through the gaps.

PLASTIC
Surfaces often need protection from water seepage, soil, or cement mix. Use plastic to line the underside of garlands, wreaths, and the insides of pots.

STRING
As well as being useful for binding materials together, string, in various colors and textures, can add a decorative element to many displays.

WREATH WRAP
This band of thin plastic can be used instead of plastic to line the back of wreaths and garlands.

PLASTIC BOWLS
To protect a container from leaks, a plastic bowl can be placed within it to hold water and flowers. A bowl can also be decorated, with rope for example, to create a surface of your own choosing.

Florist's scissors

Knife

BUTCHER'S HOOKS
When attached to the back of arrangements, hooks effectively suspend displays from mantelpieces, tables, and other surfaces.

CUTTING TOOLS
It is worth using proper florist's scissors for cutting flowers and thin wire. A knife is also useful when preparing stems, to remove bumps, and to scrape off any unwanted material.

Saucer

Plastic bowl

GLUE
Use glue to attach more awkward materials (such as shells or bulky fabric) to a display or to secure decorative material to containers.

CEMENT MIX
When mixed with water, cement powder securely holds material such as bark and logs in pots. Line the pot with plastic first.

PREPARING AND TREATING FLOWERS

BEFORE STARTING any fresh flower arrangement, it is important to prepare and treat the stems and flowers carefully to make your arrangement last longer and look better. Cleaning and cutting stems correctly encourages water uptake and makes the stems more visually attractive in a transparent container, while straightening stems gives flowers extra height and strength. Use flower food, too, whenever possible, since it contains chemicals that promote water uptake. As a last resort for really weary stems, wrap the prepared stems in paper, stand them in hot water, and add flower food.

PREPARING STEMS

1 Break off all leaves that will be below the water line. This neatens the appearance of the stems through transparent containers and helps keep the water fresh.

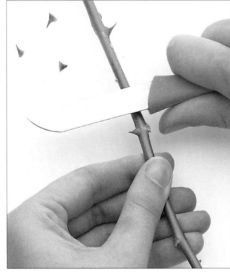

2 Now clean the stems by scraping down their length with a small knife to get rid of thorns and smooth off bumps, and remove any old plant tissue.

3 Cut stems on a slant to create a larger surface area to take up water. This also makes stems neater and easier to push into wet florist's foam and vase displays.

PLUGGING HOLLOW STEMS

1 Filling hollow-stemmed flowers (such as amaryllis) with water promotes water uptake. Hold the stems upside down and pour as much water as possible into them.

Cotton plug

2 Plug the base of the stem with cotton to keep the water in. The cotton will also allow more water to be taken into the stem once the flower is arranged.

STRAIGHTENING STEMS

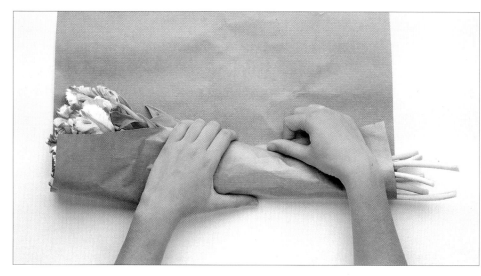

WRAP the stems in brown paper to help straighten them

1 Many flower stems need to be straightened before being arranged. Prepare the stems, wrap them in brown paper, and secure the bunch with tape or string.

2 Place the wrapped stems in plenty of fresh water and leave for a few hours, or overnight, until the stems have taken up enough water and have become straight.

CONDITIONING

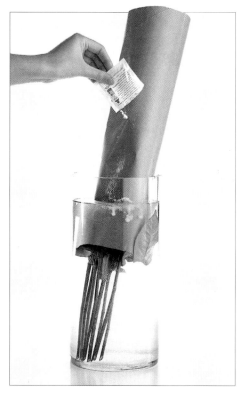

To revive drooping blooms, for example on long-stemmed roses, protect the flower heads by wrapping them in paper, stand the prepared stems in warm water, and add flower food. Leave for several hours while the warm water eliminates air locks that prevent water from reaching the heads.

KEEPING PETALS CLEAN

If flowers (such as lilies) have large, powdery stamens, they should be removed before they reach maturity to prevent them from staining the petals and surfaces. Gently pull them from their stalks with your fingers, taking care to keep them away from your clothing, since they stain badly. Lilies from florists should have stamens already removed.

SPIRALING STEMS

THE SPIRALING TECHNIQUE serves three purposes: it makes stems look attractive; creates a bunch that is practical to hold and easy to place in a vase; and provides support for stems. Spiraled and bound bouquets can simply be placed in a vase: no further arranging is necessary, since all the stems are securely held together. I like to bind stems to each other a few at a time to make the bouquet even more sturdy, instead of simply binding them all together at the end. In a spiraled vase display, stems are spiraled in the hand and remain unbound. The finished bunch is simply dropped into a container.

BOUND BOUQUET

1 *Hold the first prepared stem halfway down from the head. Hold the second stem to it, angled diagonally with its head to the left. Keep adding stems diagonally, binding with string after every third stem.*

2 *Add more flowers and foliage two or three stems at a time, following the same diagonal angle. Bind them with one turn of string only each time, to keep the "waist" of the bouquet as narrow as possible.*

3 *When the bunch is complete, tie the string in a knot or bow. Trim the stems to make the base of the bouquet flat (making it freestanding), and cover the string with complementary binding or a bow.*

HAND-HELD SPIRALED BOUQUET

1 *Hold the first prepared flower halfway down from the head. Add the second stem to it, angling it diagonally. Repeat, adding stems to the left of the previous stem.*

2 *Continue adding stems, using your thumb to keep each one secure. Make sure you place each stem at the same distance from the head as the others.*

3 *When all the flowers have been added, trim off the stems on a slant to the same length and drop the bunch into a container three-quarters full of water.*

WIRING

FLORAL WIRES IN VARIOUS GAUGES are used either to attach plant material to a base, or to wire flower heads and leaves to give them extra support. Heavier-gauge floral wires, 71 or 90 gauge, for example, are mainly used as hairpin hooks and double leg mounts to secure fairly strong items to a base. Medium-gauge wires, such as 56 gauge, can reinforce fragile dried flowers, while fine floral wires are best suited to supporting delicate flowers and leaves, or creating thin, flexible stems that can be bent to shape. Wired stems can be bound with fine florist's tape (see pages 180–181).

HAIRPIN HOOKS

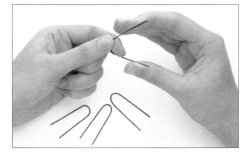

1 To bend a floral wire into a hook, hold it in the center with one hand and bend the two ends together so that they lie parallel to each other.

2 To secure plant material such as single leaves or, as shown here, a handful of moss to a base, push the hook down through the plant material into the base.

DOUBLE LEG MOUNTS

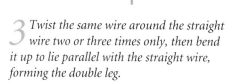

KEEP the stub wire "legs" parallel

1 Hold a floral wire horizontally behind the stem. Make sure the stem lies at the center of the wire. Bend the ends of the wire up to continue the line of the stem.

2 Take the right-hand wire and bend it across the front of the stem and over the left-hand wire. Twist it around the wire and back under the stem to the right side.

3 Twist the same wire around the straight wire two or three times only, then bend it up to lie parallel with the straight wire, forming the double leg.

WIRING A FLOWER HEAD

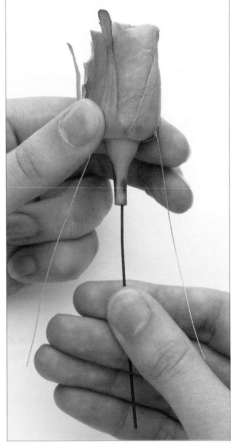

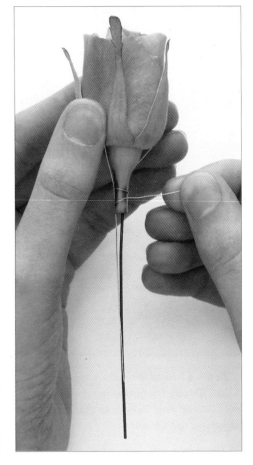

1 Cut off the stem about ½in (1cm) below the flower head. Push a heavy-gauge floral wire up the stem, into the head. Then push a fine floral wire into one side of the base of the head and out the other side.

2 Carefully pull the fine floral wire through the head so that it extends the same length on both sides. Bend the two ends down to lie parallel with the main floral wire pushed up into the flower head.

3 Pass the right-hand fine wire behind the stem and back around the left-hand fine wire and the main floral wire. Repeat twice, then bring the wire down to lie parallel with the main floral wire, and trim off the ends.

WIRING A SINGLE LEAF

WIRING A THREE-LEAFED SPRIG

1 Thread a fine wire through the main vein at the back of a leaf, a third of the way down from the top, and bend the two legs down.

2 Pass the left-hand wire leg over the stalk and twist it twice around the right-hand wire and the stalk.

1 Wire the right-hand and middle leaf on the stem individually, as for a single leaf, then trim off the wire legs.

2 Wire the remaining left-hand leaf, as before, then twist the left-hand leg around the stem and the other wire legs.

WIRING OTHER FLOWERS AND FOLIAGE

DELPHINIUM
The individual flowers on delphinium stems can be wired for use in delicate arrangements. Push a fine floral wire through the stalk below the flower and twist into a double leg mount.

NERINE
Cut the stem ½in (1cm) below the flower head. Push a fine floral wire through the base of the flower head and twist around the short stem to form a double leg mount.

DRIED ACHILLEA
To secure achillea into dry foam in dried displays, remove sprigs from the main stem, and bind two or three sprigs together with a medium-gauge floral wire bent into a double leg mount.

FREESIA
To wire freesias you will need a reel of florist's wire, because fine floral wires are too short. Cut the stem ½in (1cm) below the main flower, and starting at the base of the stem, coil the wire around the flower, winding it up between each bud. Wind the wire back down around the buds to the starting point and twist into a double leg mount.

PARROT TULIP
Push a long, heavy-gauge floral wire up the stem of the tulip. Cover another long floral wire with fine florist's tape, leaving ¾in (2cm) uncovered. Push the uncovered end into the stem below the head and into the flower head. Then wind the covered wire down around the stem and twist around the wire pushed into the stem to form a double leg mount.

LILY-OF-THE-VALLEY LEAF
Push a heavy-gauge wire up the stem. Thread fine floral wire through the central vein at the back of the leaf, a third of the way from the top. Bend both ends down, and thread through the vein, a third of the way down again, so that the wires cross. Bring the ends of the wires down and twist into a double leg mount.

DAISY HEAD
Cut the stem ¾in (2cm) below the head, then push a heavy-gauge floral wire up the stem and into the head. Thread a fine floral wire through the base of the flower and twist it to form a double leg mount.

GLADIOLUS
Individual buds can be removed from a gladiolus stem and wired. Push a heavy-gauge floral wire up into the flower head, thread a fine floral wire through the bud, and twist it into a double leg mount.

BINDING WIRED STEMS

WIRED FLOWERS AND LEAVES are often bound with green fine florist's tape to conceal the wires and make the flowers easier to work with. Fine florist's tape is flexible, light, and seals with pressure and heat, making it quick and easy to use. The tape can also be used to bind together a number of ready-wired and bound flowers and foliage. When binding particularly delicate elements, such as for a headdress or a wedding bouquet, I split the tape down its length to make it even finer to work with.

BINDING SINGLE STEMS

Hold the end of the fine florist's tape against the top of the wired stem, just under the leaf, and revolve the stem so that the tape winds down around the wires, overlapping itself. Twist off the tape firmly with your fingers to seal it at the end of the wires.

TAPE attached just below the leaf

FULLY wired stem

COMBINING BOUND ITEMS

SECOND LEAF attached and bent into shape

1 Hold the wired and bound leaf against a wired and bound flower stem. Press the end of the fine florist's tape below the flower head, and revolve the flower and leaf so that the tape binds them together. Wire and bind another leaf.

2 Place the second leaf against the front of the main stem, and revolve the group so that the fine florist's tape binds the entire length of the stems. Twist the tape to seal at the end and bend the second leaf to the required angle.

MAKING A UNIT

Units made up of several individually wired and bound elements attached along a main stem with fine florist's tape can be combined to form a larger arrangement, for example the Shower Bouquet on pages 100–105. The bound elements backtrack along the main stem because you work from the top down, always attaching elements below the previous item, rather than grouping them around a central flower (as in a boutonniere).

1 Wire and bind the longest element being used. This sets the length of the whole unit. Hold the next wired and bound component to it at the point of binding on both stems. Tape them together with a few twists of fine florist's tape, making sure both stems stay parallel.

2 To add more wired and bound components, work toward you, backtracking from the last attached item down the main stem. Bind on the next component, here a lily-of-the-valley flower, immediately below the binding point of the last item, the ivy, on the right of the stem.

3 Keep binding on wired and bound components, alternating from right to left down the main stem, and binding immediately below the last item with a few twists of tape. Keep all the stems parallel, not twisted, to reduce bulk and keep the stems neat.

4 When you have added enough components to fill the length of the unit, bind all the stems together with tape to form a handle. Twist off the tape to seal it at the end of the stems. This unit can now be attached to others to form a larger arrangement.

MAKING BOWS

BOWS MADE FROM RIBBON OR FABRIC can enliven many types of display and add movement to dried flower arrangements. Single and double bows are easy to make and simple to attach to a base with double leg mounts (see page 177). Binding the stem of a posy with complementary ribbon and finishing it with a decorative knot lends a professional look to the completed bouquet.

SINGLE BOW

1 Gather the fabric in the center with your left hand. Take the right tail back to the center to form a loop. Hold the central point in your right hand.

2 Take an equal amount of fabric from the left tail and bring it to the center to form a second loop. Hold the central point in your left hand.

3 Hold a heavy-gauge floral wire vertically behind the central point. Bend the top of the wire over and twist to form a double leg mount (see page 177).

4 Cut the ends of the fabric to the desired length on a slant, then use the wires of the double leg mount to press the bow into the base of the display.

DOUBLE BOW

1 Using twice the amount of fabric, follow steps 1 and 2 above. Then bring the right-hand tail back to the center to form a second loop.

2 Holding the central point in your right hand, bring some fabric from the left-hand tail back to the central point to form another loop on the left side.

3 Loop a short length of fabric over the central point, then wind a heavy-gauge floral wire around its tails to form a double leg mount (see page 177).

4 Trim off the tails on the central piece of fabric. Cut the tails of the bow on a slant, and use the double leg mount to hook the bow to a base.

BINDING A POSY

CUT THE ENDS of the ribbon on a slant

1 Leaving an adequate tail, bind the ribbon around the top of the stems, spiraling it downward to overlap itself.

2 At the bottom of the stems, tuck the ribbon under the end of the stems and press it up against the side of the posy.

3 Bind the ribbon back up around the stem, securing the tuck at the bottom. Again, spiral and overlap the ribbon.

4 When you reach the starting point, tie the ends of ribbon in a knot, and cut the tails to the required length on a slant.

PRESERVING PLANT MATERIAL

FLOWERS SHOULD BE PRESERVED as quickly as possible to prevent materials from decaying or colors fading in the process. I generally air dry most flowers and foliage, but silica gel and glycerin are more appropriate for some plant materials: lilies, for example, can be preserved only with silica gel, and glycerin helps flowers to retain their suppleness, but can cause radical color variations. Silica gel and glycerin are available at craft stores and sometimes at florists.

AIR DRYING

Pick flowers in dry weather a few days before they reach their prime. Remove the lower leaves and spiral the stems to create as much space between the flower heads as possible for air to circulate. Bind the bunches with string and hang them in a warm, well-ventilated dark room for about a week.

GLYCERIN

Glycerin suits woody-stemmed flowers and foliage. The material will remain supple but can undergo extreme color changes in the process. Make a solution of 50% hot water and 50% glycerin in a vase, then stand the stems in it for at least a week before removing and washing them.

SILICA GEL

FLOWERS laid in gel before being covered completely

Silica draws out moisture from plants, leaving them looking very similar to fresh flowers. Pour a layer of gel into a lidded container, place the flowers on it, and completely cover them with more gel. Close the lid, seal it with tape, and leave for a week or more.

A GLOSSARY OF FLOWERS

THE VARIETY AND ABUNDANCE of plants available are truly inspiring and a constant source of delight, but selection from such a wealth of materials can be daunting. A listing follows of the plants featured in this book with details of their physical characteristics and suitability for different styles of arrangement. Information on life span, availability, and drying is also included.

FLOWERS

The color and form of flowers should suit the container you wish to use and the final location of the finished display. Blooms should also be compatible with other flowers and foliage in the arrangement.

Acacia
MIMOSA
Yellow, ball-shaped clusters of flowers with a lovely scent, particularly suited to spring arrangements. Short life span. See pages 86–89.

Achillea filipendulina 'Gold Plate'
ACHILLEA
Vibrant gold-colored flower heads that mark the onset of summer and bring to life the blues, oranges, reds, and pinks of country-style displays. Easy to grow. Flowers retain their color after drying. See pages 36–39, 86–89, 136–137, 141, 158–159.

Achillea ptarmica 'The Pearl'
ACHILLEA
Large heads of tiny white flowers and tapering dark green leaves. Dries well and creates strong architectural shapes when massed together. Excellent filler flowers when used fresh. See pages 143, 148–151, 156–157, 179.

Aconitum
MONKSHOOD
Tall spikes of blue, white, or cream hooded flowers that look wonderful in country mixes or on their own in more modern displays. See pages 82–85.

Amaranthus
AMARANTHUS
Love-lies-bleeding (*Amaranthus caudatus*) has dramatic tendrils of velvety crimson or green flowers, guaranteed to cause a stir whenever they are used. Other forms of amaranthus are denser and more upright. See pages 19, 82–85, 138–141.

Anemone
ANEMONE
Bright, cheerful flowers in strong red, blue, and purple hues. Mixed with other foliage and flowers, they have a nostalgic, almost Victorian, feel. Mass tightly in a plain container for a simple modern look. See pages 43, 54–55.

Angelica archangelica
ANGELICA
Large white or green domes of flowers and bright green foliage. Mixed with foliage, they have a country-type, herbaceous feel. For a bolder, modern look, display in strong, sculptural containers. See pages 86–89.

Antirrhinum
SNAPDRAGON
Clusters of flowers in a wide array of colors with an old-fashioned appeal. Classed as a garden flower but can be used in modern, as well as country-style, displays. Short-lived in water. See pages 30–33, 36–39, 58–59.

Asclepias tuberosa
BUTTERFLY WEED
Small, bright orange-red flowers with long, lance-shaped leaves. Best combined with other flowers. See pages 44–47.

Aster
MICHAELMAS DAISY
Tall pink, white, or violet daisies with yellow or orange centers. These flowers flit in and out of fashion. They create a sense of nostalgia and evoke a country feel. See pages 82–85.

Astilbe
ASTILBE
Tapering plumes of feathery flowers ranging in color from white and pale pink to cherry pink and deep blood red. Since the shape is quite pointed, it is best to combine astilbe with rounder, fuller blooms. Dries well. See pages 15, 58–59.

Atriplex
ATRIPLEX
Plume-shaped groups of bobbles in deep red or bright green. Atriplex should be combined with other flowers. Dries exceptionally well. See pages 146, 156–157.

Calendula officinalis
POT MARIGOLD
Fluorescent yellow or glowing orange flowers, with a childlike simplicity and herbal scent. They look rustic and cottagey in a country jug but more modern *en masse* in glass tanks. See page 21.

Centaurea cyanus
CORNFLOWER
Delicate, almost wild-looking flowers in pink, blue, mauve, and white. Mixed with other perennials, such as scabiosa and peonies, they have a country-type image. The vibrant blue variety used alone in simple glass vases has a modern appeal. Available all year, but best in summer. See pages 14, 21.

Consolida
LARKSPUR
Gentle blooms in a range of pastel pink, blue, and white that add a rustic touch to most displays, especially when mixed with cornflowers, roses and summery foliage in country-style containers. Short life span. Dries well. See pages 13, 30–33, 162–163.

Convallaria
LILY-OF-THE-VALLEY
Charming bells of white or pink flowers with a sweet, delicate fragrance. A traditional favorite for wedding bouquets. Can now be bought throughout the year. Lasts well in water. See pages 96–97, 100–105, 179.

Craspedia
CRASPEDIA
Bright yellow, perfectly rounded, compact globes of flowers on long, leafless stems. They look distinctive in bouquets and posies and are most commonly available as dried flowers. See pages 158–159.

Cynara cardunculus
CARDOON
Large, thistlelike, purplish flower heads rising out of clumps of pointed, silver-gray leaves. Provide interesting textural contrast and strong patches of color in displays. Flower heads dry very well. See pages 92–93.

Dahlia
DAHLIA
Long-stemmed flowers in a range of shapes and colors, including white, red, mauve, yellow and orange. A popular choice for a wide variety of arrangements,

providing extravagant splashes of color that enliven the dullest of surroundings. Long-lasting in water. See pages 15, 20, 30–33.

Delphinium
DELPHINIUM
Tall spires of flowers in various shades of blue or red with dark or white centers. Particularly impressive displayed in tall, elegant vases or mixed with country border flowers such as astilbe, lupines, peonies, and foxgloves. Dries well. See pages 14, 20–21, 58–59, 179.

Dianthus
PINK, CARNATION
Frilly-edged and fragrant flowers in myriad colors, some with contrasting eyes. With their nostalgic associations, pinks have a charming, old-fashioned look when massed in jugs or vases. Long-lasting in water. See page 15.

Erica
HEATHER
Small shrublike plants with green or bronze foliage and clusters of white, pink, or purple flowers. Combine well with ornamental cabbages and cut flowers such as lavender roses. Available as plants and cut flowers through the autumn. See pages 60–61, 66–68, 78–81, 100–105, 108–109.

Eryngium
SEA HOLLY
Spiky, thistlelike flowers in silvery blue or green. The harsh texture suits dramatic, modern arrangements, and provides striking contrast for softer blooms. See pages 58–59, 96.

Eustoma grandiflorum
LISIANTHUS, PRAIRIE GENTIAN
Delicate trumpets of white, cream, lilac, pink, purple, or bicolored flowers in single and double-petaled varieties. Elegant pastel pink, or white and lilac bicolored types, have a soft, feminine feel when mixed with sweet peas or roses. Long-lasting in water. See pages 21, 39, 92–93.

Freesia
FREESIA
Trumpet-shaped, highly scented waxy flowers in a wide range of colors. For a vibrant display, use a rich mix of colors, or choose large bunches of one color for a simpler, stylish effect. Blue freesias have a shorter life span, and yellow or cream flowers have a stronger scent. Long-lasting in water. See pages 98–99, 179.

Gardenia
GARDENIA
Ivory or white flowers in single or double varieties with a heady, rich, and exotic perfume and a simple, elegant form. Effective as house plants, they are also stylish and romantic in boutonnieres and wedding bouquets. Flowers are easily bruised and should be handled with care. See pages 96–97, 100–105.

Genista
BROOM
Lovely arching stems of small, scented flowers now available in many colors, including white, pink, peach, and yellow. Combine with spring flowers such as narcissi or tulips, or display on their own. See pages 56–57, 86–89.

Gerbera
GERBERA
Daisy-shaped flowers with a fresh, cheerful look, in brilliant, even garish, colors, including cream, yellow, orange, red, pink, or brown. Particularly suitable for large-scale arrangements or vase displays where the vibrant colors can boldly clash together. Long-lasting. See page 97.

Gladiolus
GLADIOLUS
Tall, slightly arching stems of brightly colored flowers with swordlike leaves. Massed in a tall vase, they take on a stately appearance. Avoid using them to form a triangular shape with a spear at each point. Long-lasting. See pages 51, 179.

Helenium
SNEEZEWEED
Wild-looking sprays of yellow, orange, or brown daisylike flower heads with prominent centers. With their summery, country-style charm, they are best used *en masse* in a rustic jug or mixed with flowers such as red-hot pokers and sunflowers. Quite long-lasting. See pages 62–63, 106–107.

Helianthus
SUNFLOWER
Very tall, large-headed flowers with golden yellow petals radiating from a large, dark center. Grouped in an earthenware vase, they have rustic, old-fashioned connotations, but are also impressive when set against richly colored flowers and foliage in modern displays. See pages 12–13, 19, 94–95, 120–123, 128–129, 146–147.

Helichrysum bracteatum
STRAWFLOWER
Vividly colored rounded flower heads with papery bracts instead of petals. Firmly established as dried flowers and rarely used fresh, they create eye-catching blocks of color when clumped together. Easy to grow. See pages 19, 119, 129, 134–135.

Hippeastrum
AMARYLLIS
Large, fleshy, lilylike blooms on tall stems in red, apricot, white, or pink. Used alone in tall glass vases, the flowers have an austere air. When cut down low and surrounded with glossy foliage, such as camellia leaves, they have a stylish, elegant quality. See pages 51, 54–57, 174.

Hyacinthus
HYACINTH
Heavy spikes of highly scented flowers in many colors that can be used as pot plants or cut flowers. For a spring arrangement, combine with flowers such as narcissi or tulips, or use on their own to maximize their bold, sculptural shape. See pages 43, 65.

Hydrangea macrophylla
MOP-HEADED HYDRANGEA
Bushy mops of flower heads in sugary whites, lilacs, and pinks, and burnished autumnal reds. Combine with open, fleshy roses in summer, and rose hips, lilies, and gerberas in autumn. The rounded heads help define the shape of a display and add volume. Easy to grow and long-lasting. See pages 14, 39, 44–47, 59, 65, 82–85, 106–107, 160–161, 164–165.

Hypericum
HYPERICUM
Saucer-shaped, golden yellow flowers throughout the summer and amber-toned, or even pinkish, berries in autumn. Use with other autumnal-colored flowers, such as lilies and roses. See pages 30–33, 40–43, 95.

Jasminum
JASMINE
Flowing tendrils of white, star-shaped flowers in summer and clusters of yellow flowers in winter with a strong, sweet fragrance. Incorporate in bridal bouquets for a delicate, feminine touch, and use the supple foliage to trail out from country displays. See pages 58–59.

Kniphofia
RED-HOT POKER
Tall, eye-catching spires of glowing red, orange, or yellow flowers with strong stems. Their bold shape, color and height make an immediate impact in textural displays. They have a very short season but are well worth using throughout the autumn. Not long-lasting. See pages 106–107.

Lachenalia
CAPE COWSLIP
Bulbous plants with hanging bells of red, yellow, orange, or green flowers that can be bought as plants and occasionally as cut flowers. If you prefer to display lachenalia in vases, it is better to grow this flower yourself since it is not often available in florist shops. See page 22.

Lavandula
LAVENDER
Fine spikes of highly fragrant white, pink, or mauve flowers with silvery gray leaves. An English favorite, especially when dried, lavender strikes a note of nostalgia when mixed with other flowers and is stylishly modern when bunched on its own. See pages 18, 119, 126–128, 146–147, 156–157.

Lilium
LILY
Majestic, fragrant flowers in myriad colors and forms, often trumpet-shaped or with strong, curled-back petals. Now losing their morbid associations, lilies suit a variety of small or large-scale displays. Remove stamens as buds begin to open since the pollen can stain clothes and furniture. See pages 62–63, 91, 175, 183.

Narcissus
DAFFODIL
Popular spring bulbs with trumpets of yellow, orange, or white flowers, sometimes in miniature form. Use massed on their own for fresh, spring displays, team with foliage and branches for textural arrangements, or pot for attractive planted displays. Many varieties are fragrant. See pages 40–43, 65, 70–71, 86–89.

Nerine sarniensis
GUERNSEY LILY
Autumnal bulbous plants with clusters of pink, orange, or white curly, trumpetlike flowers. Combine with vibrant orange and pink roses or use the white variety to create a monochromatic display with other white flowers. See page 179.

Paeonia
PEONY
Large, fleshy single or double blooms in white, yellow, pink, or red. They look equally impressive displayed singly in a vase, cut short for centerpieces, or massed in jugs, urns, or baskets in voluptuous rustic displays. See pages 120–123, 146, 152–153.

Papaver
POPPY
Delicate flowers with tissuelike petals in bright or pastel tones. The more vibrant varieties complement gerbera and coppery foliages, while softer creams, apricots, and pinks blend well with other pastel-colored flowers. Pods are easy to dry and spray-paint different colors. See pages 19, 40–43, 128, 134, 138–141, 143, 146, 148–151.

Physalis alkekengi
CHINESE LANTERN
Brilliant orange paper lanterns containing fruit. Most commonly seen and used dried, they have a striking impact when used fresh during the autumn harvest period. Mix with natural wheat and foliage for an autumnal feel or combine with clashing blue for a bold, modern look. See pages 164–165.

Primula vulgaris
PRIMROSE
Short-stemmed, flat, creamy yellow flowers with dark eyes. Their natural woodland habitat makes them suitable for country displays, clustered together in jugs or bowls. A delightful choice for planted arrangements in spring. See pages 74–75.

Prunus
CHERRY
Elegant branches with sprays of white, pink, or red spring flowers. For a tall, architectural display, use alone. See pages 44–47.

Ranunculus
BUTTERCUP
Brightly colored single or double blooms with layer upon layer of feathery, papery petals. Multi-colored bunches suit modern or rustic surroundings. Long-lasting. See page 22.

Rosa
ROSE
A wide variety of colors and sizes, the majority with thorny stems. Large-headed, open roses in orange, pink, and yellow produce a rich, country garden look, while displays of single colors have a more formal image. Dried roses retain their scent and color well and are a versatile ingredient in dried displays. See pages 10, 15, 18, 20, 30–39, 44–49, 58–63, 66–69, 86–89, 92–93, 95, 98–105, 118, 124–125, 130–131, 134–5, 138–142, 146, 156–161, 166.

Rosa eglanteria
ROSEHIP, SWEET BRIAR
Cupped, single, pink flowers in midsummer suit casual, rustic displays. The red hips in autumn create wonderful fluid lines when mixed with foliage or used alone. See pages 60–61, 92–93.

Scabiosa
SCABIOSA
Soft, ruffled flowers in blue, mauve, crimson, or white. Lime green bobbled centers slowly bursting into pink and white "pins" have a simple, unaffected appeal. Quite long-lasting in water. See page 21.

Scilla
SCILLA
A collection of scented, star-shaped blue, violet, or white flowers on delicate stems. Not to be confused with English bluebells. Some of these wild flowers are now grown commercially and complement other spring flowers. Short-lived as cut flowers. See page 70.

Sedum
STONECROP
Succulent plants with flat, dense heads of red, pink, or mauve flowers. Smaller varieties have white or yellow flowers. With their curious texture, they are very useful filler and recessionary flowers. Extremely long-lasting in water. See pages 108–109.

Stephanotis floribunda
STEPHANOTIS, WAX FLOWER
Small clusters of waxy, scented white flowers set against glossy, dark green leaves. Easily trained around wire frames, making attractive pot plants. Flowers bruise easily and are best for short-lived displays, such as bridal head-dresses. See pages 100–105.

Syringa
LILAC
Plumes of fragrant flowers in white and various shades of mauve and purple. Commercially grown varieties arrive without foliage or fragrance, so it is best to incorporate the flowers into displays or use when naturally available in abundance. See pages 58–59, 98–99.

Tulipa
TULIP
Elegant, waxy flowers in myriad colors and markings. For a simple, modern display, arrange in a clear glass vase to take advantage of the graceful stems. Available most of the year but best in winter and spring. See pages 25, 40–43, 52–53, 96–97, 179.

Viburnum
VIBURNUM
Evergreen and deciduous shrubs with white or pink flowers. Full, pale green blossoms enhance spring lemons and creams, as well as summer blues and pinks. Available commercially from early spring until early summer, when their natural season begins. See pages 60–61, 98–99.

Viola x *wittrockiana*
PANSY
Short-stemmed, velvety flowers often with eye-catching contrasting patches of color. The delicate, open faces create nostalgic displays but are short-lived. See pages 66–69, 78–81.

Zantedeschia
CALLA LILY
Supremely elegant, pure white, yellow, or pink trumpets with a central spike and glossy surface. Epitomizing 1930s glamour and a simplicity of style, these lilies are too pure to mess with and are best displayed alone. Long-lasting in water. See pages 14–15, 21.

HERBS

With their aromatic scent, leaf variations, and simplicity of style, herbs make ideal filler foliage and suit planted displays.

Anethum graveolens
DILL
Finely cut, feathery leaves with an aromatic fragrance. Impart a soft country look to any display and rarely used alone. The flower heads are just as attractive when gone to seed. See pages 33, 44–47.

Helichrysum italicum
CURRY PLANT
Clusters of small, bright yellow flower heads and silvery gray leaves. Valuable for texture, color, and scent, and perfect for wiring in wedding bouquets and head-dresses. See pages 72–73.

Hyssopus officinalis
HYSSOP
Aromatic, semi-evergreen or deciduous bushy shrub with pointed, deep green leaves. Small clusters of white, pink, or blue flowers from midsummer to early autumn. Incorporate into fresh herb arrangements or use the dried flowers and leaves in potpourri. See pages 72–73.

Laurus nobilis
BAY
Oval, glossy leaves that can be used fresh or dry and have a sweet, aromatic scent. Their leathery surface is interesting for textural contrast. See page 168.

Mentha
MINT
Mid- to bright green leaves with an invigorating scent. Useful as filler foliage in arrangements to lend textural variety and a fresh aroma. See pages 95–96.

Origanum
MARJORAM, OREGANO
Small green leaves and mauve, pink, or white flowers. Noted for its distinctive aroma, this herb suits mixed country-style displays. See pages 72–73, 132–133.

Rosmarinus officinalis
ROSEMARY
Bushy shrub with needlelike green and silvery leaves and blue flowers in spring. Its long-lasting quality and traditional associations make it ideal for wedding work. The dried leaves can be added to potpourri. See pages 16, 72–73.

Salvia
SAGE
Highly scented gray-green, purple, or yellow leaves make a charming contribution to wedding head-dresses and bouquets. Long-lasting. See pages 72–73.

FOLIAGE

Foliage is invaluable for creating strong outlines and movement in displays, as well as providing textural contrast and acting as filler material.

Acer
MAPLE
An array of trees and shrubs with foliage ranging from deeply cut purple leaves to fan-shaped green leaves edged with yellow. Useful for color contrast and as a sturdy filler foliage. See pages 30–33.

Aesculus hippocastanum
HORSE CHESTNUT
Sticky buds in spring are followed by voluptuous foliage and blossoms in summer that can be displayed on their own. Shiny fruit ("buckeyes") encased in prickly shells suit autumnal or harvest displays. See pages 108–109.

Alchemilla mollis
LADY'S MANTLE
I tend to use this as a foliage. Tiny lime green flowers and dark green leaves offset pinks and oranges. Perfect for wedding displays and fresh flower arrangements. Long-lasting. See pages 36–39, 94–95.

Bupleurum fruticosum
SHRUBBY HARE'S EAR
Bushy shrub with slender shoots, dark glossy foliage, and small, yellow flowers. Provides interesting color contrast and is an attractive filler. See page 17.

Cornus
DOGWOOD
Upright shrub with red stems and red shoots in winter. Effective when combined with red lilies, copper beech, and red tulips. Equally impressive tied in bundles and left freestanding or used as a trellis around potted bulbs. See pages 34–35, 40–43.

Cotinus coggygria
SMOKE TREE
Deep purple leaves with a simple rounded shape. Ideal for rich, velvety arrangements, especially when combined with red and orange material. See pages 60–61.

Cotoneaster
COTONEASTER
Wonderful autumn foliage with dark shiny leaves, heavily laden with red berries. Particularly striking when combined with red lilies or incorporated into autumnal displays. See pages 82–85, 108–109.

Dasylirion
BEAR GRASS
Slender, glossy green, arching tendrils with a linear, modern look. Combine with sculptural flowers such as lilies and amaryllis for a strong, stylish display. See page 17.

Eucalyptus
EUCALYPTUS
Silvery blue, aromatic foliage available in many leaf shapes and a wide range of colors. Although inexpensive, it has a sophisticated, stylish image especially when used architecturally with lilies or amaryllis. The bronze-leaved variety complements orange, red, and yellow flowers. See pages 16, 52–55, 60–61, 92–93, 114–115, 134–135.

Euphorbia
MILKWEED, SPURGE
Yellow or green blooms add spice to many kinds of displays, particularly when set against orange, pink, cream, and yellow flowers. Long-lasting. See page 24.

Fagus sylvatica f. *purpurea*
COPPER BEECH
Deep purple, oval leaves. Look wonderful teamed with pink peonies, roses, and pinks in the summer months. Do not use too early in the season: the young leaves wither quickly. See page 17.

Hebe
HEBE
Evergreen shrubs with dense spikes of blue, white, or pink flowers and small, fleshy leaves. A welcome choice when other foliage begins to disappear in autumn. See pages 40–43.

Hedera
IVY
Vigorous, evergreen, self-clinging climbers in a large range of shapes and colors, from dark green to butter yellow. Trailing stems lend a natural fluidity to displays. See pages 16, 30–33, 43, 62–64, 78–89, 96–105, 108–109, 114.

Hosta
PLANTAIN LILY
Large heart or lance-shaped leaves in varying shades of green, yellow, and grayish blue. There are many variegated forms. Flowers are white, lilac-blue, or purple. Useful in a wide array of displays, including as edging for posies. See pages 16, 94–95.

Ilex
HOLLY
Glossy green or variegated spiny leaves with clusters of yellow, red, or black berries. Traditionally used at Christmas. Combines well with reds to highlight red berries against dark leaves, or with whites and creams if leaves are variegated. Long-lasting and available all year. See pages 34–35, 96–97, 110–115.

Laurelia
LAUREL
Oval, shiny dark green leaves with white bobbles of flowers in spring. A good year-round foliage that is invaluable at Christmas for use in wreaths and green-based arrangements. Extremely long-lasting. See pages 96–97.

Leucadendron
LEUCADENDRON
Strong, smooth leaves with sculptural conelike flowers. The red-tinted variety is useful in festive arrangements throughout autumn and winter. See pages 34–35.

Ligustrum
PRIVET
Common foliage plant with narrow, oval-shaped mid- or lime green leaves. Some varieties have white flowers in summer followed by black berries. Combine with avant-garde flowers for striking effects. Easy to grow. See pages 94–95.

Magnolia
MAGNOLIA
Deciduous and evergreen shrubs and trees with white or soft pink flowers. Glycerin-preserved leaves can be dyed deep green or russet. Perfect for long-lasting dried festive displays. See pages 151, 167.

Myrica gale
SWEET GALE, BOG MYRTLE
Red-stemmed, with reddish green leaves. An attractive winter filler foliage for country-style and festive displays. See pages 114–115.

Picea abies
NORWAY SPRUCE
Fast-growing conifers with dark green, needlelike leaves and glossy brown cones. Often used as Christmas trees; sprigs are useful for festive displays. See pages 110–113.

Quercus
OAK
Deciduous or evergreen trees and shrubs with a variety of leaf shapes

and colors. Summer foliage turns amber or reddish brown in autumn, making it ideal for harvest displays. See pages 82–85.

Ruscus
BUTCHER'S BROOM
Dark green leaves with yellow or scarlet berries. Relatively stiff and upright, the stems create strong outlines in vase displays and larger arrangements. Incredibly tough and long-lasting. See page 17.

Senecio x *hybridus*
CINERARIA
Silvery, antler-shaped leaves that bring a delicate, wintry effect to displays. Combine with white flowers in wedding bouquets and use for color contrast. See pages 56–57, 65, 97, 100–105.

Senecio 'Sunshine'
SENECIO
Silvery gray foliage, felted leaves, and clusters of yellow daisylike flowers. Has a frosty appearance when teamed with white flowers, and takes on a gentle, feminine look with pinks and blues. See pages 39, 44–47.

Skimmia japonica
SKIMMIA
Evergreen, bushy shrubs with glossy leaves and dense clusters of small white flowers followed by red berries. Effective with other red flowers. Long-lasting. See pages 44–47.

Stachys lanata
LAMB'S-EARS
Soft, downy, silvery leaves and pale pink flowers on gray stems. Delicate and feminine when mixed with pinks and blues; rather old-fashioned looking when combined with country garden flowers. Dries well, retaining the soft texture. See pages 143, 146.

Stephanandra
STEPHANANDRA
Delicate-looking shrub with deeply toothed, pale green triangular leaves that turn golden yellow in autumn. See pages 44–47.

MOSSES AND LICHENS

Mosses and lichens are used as decorative fillers in dried or fresh arrangements or as attractive bases in potted or basket displays.

Cladonia
LICHEN
Silvery gray plant used in its dry form to impart color highlights and textural contrast to displays. See pages 48, 70, 110–113, 128, 135, 141, 143, 149.

Grimmia pulvinata
BUN MOSS
Beautiful, bright green moss that grows in compact clumps. Use fresh to make the most of its rich texture and color. See pages 66–69, 71, 78–81, 124–125, 129.

Sphagnum
SPHAGNUM MOSS
A loose, tendrilly moss. Useful for filling wreaths and to add trailing elements and filler material to arrangements. See pages 78–81, 86–89, 110–115, 138–141, 144–145, 148–151, 162–163.

Mnium
SHEET MOSS
Rich green, velvety moss. Useful as a surface ingredient, being more compact than sphagnum moss. See pages 36–39, 74–75, 86–89, 120–123, 129, 136–139, 151, 162–163, 166, 168–169.

VEGETABLES AND CROPS

Particularly appropriate for rustic, autumnal arrangements, vegetables and crops introduce a fresh, natural element into more traditional displays.

Brassica oleracea
ORNAMENTAL CABBAGE
Attractive, curly-edged cabbages available in a range of tones from

white to purple. They can be combined with other fruit and vegetables, and the purple variety is particularly striking set against blue and purplish flowers. See pages 10, 48–49, 78–85.

Cynara scolymus
GLOBE ARTICHOKE
Globelike green or blue flowers with a rather brutish appearance. Always makes a bold statement. Can be dried and the bracts brightened with delicate highlights of gold paint. See pages 18, 54–55, 113, 124–125, 143, 147, 168.

Humulus lupulus
HOPS
Green, yellow, or variegated serrated leaves and small green flowerlike bracts that later develop into hops. Instant garlands for Thanksgiving tables. Dried hops suspended from ceilings or incorporated in dried flower baskets make excellent, permanent decorations. See pages 164–165.

Phleum pratense
TIMOTHY
Soft, feathery pale green seedheads and thin, tapering leaves. Useful when dried and incorporated in dried hanging bunches or textural displays to soften harsher surfaces and offset more sculptural flowers. See pages 12–13, 94, 129, 143, 147.

Triticum aestivum
WHEAT
Grasslike crop with large seedheads. Can be used fresh or dried and is particularly suitable for Thanksgiving or autumnal displays. See pages 138–141, 144–145, 164–165.

Zea mays
CORN
Tall, strong plants with large golden seedheads sheathed in husks with a lining of silklike threads. The strong, sculptural shape makes a dramatic statement in dried arrangements. Particularly suitable for harvest displays. See pages 12–13, 18, 143, 147, 164.

INDEX

AUTHOR'S ACKNOWLEDGMENTS
I would like to thank everyone at my shop in James Street for their support throughout the book, particularly Donna, Michele, Mark, and Emma who worked on the photographic sessions.

Of course, without the incredible help of Tracey and Stefanie at Dorling Kindersley this book just would not have happened. My grateful thanks also to Dave King for his wonderful photography, not to mention his fantastic lunches.

There is, of course, a whole team of people at Dorling Kindersley working hard in the background, and my thanks to them for their fine work.

Thanks also to The Real Health Store, Clifton Road, Maida Vale, London, W9, for the loan of Ralph Curry's wooden bowl.

PUBLISHER'S ACKNOWLEDGMENTS
Dorling Kindersley would like to thank Deborah Swallow for design assistance; Lorna Damms for editorial assistance; Helen Gatward for hand modeling; Jonathan Buckley for photographic assistance; Donna, Mark, Michele, Emma, and everyone at Jane Packer Flowers; Texas Home Care for the mantelpiece on pages 78-81.
Illustrations: Karen Ruane **Index:** Ella Skene